Dollars & Sense-Abilities for Business Owners

Christy Wilson

PUBLISHED BY IME Publishing Group DISCLAIMER AND/OR LEGAL NOTICES

While all attempts have been made to verify the information provided in this book and its ancillary materials, neither the author or the publisher assume any responsibility for errors, inaccuracies or omissions and is not responsible for any financial loss by consumer in any manner. Any slights of people or organizations are unintentional. If advice concerning legal, financial, accounting or related matters is needed, the service of a qualified professional should be sought. This book and its associated axillary materials, including verbal and written training, is not intended for use as a source of legal, financial or accounting advice. You should be aware of the various laws governing business transactions or other business practices in your particular geographical location.

EARNINGS AND INCOME DISCLAIMER

With respect to the reliability, accuracy, timeliness, usefulness, adequacy, completeness, and/or suitability of information provided in the book, Christy Wilson and IME Publishing Group its Partners Associates Affiliates Consultants and/or presenters make no warranties guarantees representations or claims of any kind. Readers' results will vary depending on a number of factors. Any and all claims or representations as to income earnings are not to be considered and average earnings. Testimonials are not representative. This book and all products and services are for education and informational purposes only. Use caution and see the advice of qualified professionals. Check with your accountant, attorney or professional adviser before acting on this or any information. You agreed that Christy Wilson and IME Publishing Group is not responsible for the success or failure of your personal, business, health or financial decisions relating to any information presented by Christy Wilson and IME Publishing Group or Company products/ services. Earnings potentials is entirely dependent on the efforts, skills and application of the individual person. Exercises and ideas in the information materials offered are simply opinion or experience, and thus should not be misinterpreted as promises, typical results or guarantees (expressed or implied). The author and the publisher Christy Wilson, IME Publishing Group (IME or any IME Representatives) Shall in no way, under any circumstances be held liable to any party (or third-party) for any direct, indirect, punitive, special, incidental or other consequential damages arising directly or indirectly from any use of books, materials and or seminar trainings, which is provided *as is*, and without warranties Christy Wilson/IME Publishing Group.

IME Publishing Group

1990 N California Blvd. Suite 20 PMB 1065 Walnut Creek, California 94596

1-866-726-6563

www.IMEPublishingGroup.com

Christy Wilson-1st ed.

Stop Procrastination and Start Seeing Results

Feeling stuck? This guide is your go-to for tackling procrastination head-on. Discover practical, easy-to-follow steps to stop putting things off and start making real growth progress in your business. Perfect for those who want to turn their intentions into actions and see immediate results. Get ready to move forward with clarity and confidence!

http://bit.ly/4d4r5dZ

Table of Contents

Chapter 1 Introduction

The Magic Behind the Million-Mark

Welcome to *Dollars & Sense-Abilities for Business Owners.* Christy Wilson here, and I'm so excited to start. I want you to begin by imagining yourself walking into a room and instantly being able to connect with everyone you meet. Picture yourself navigating complex negotiations quickly and understanding what drives the person sitting across from you. This skill would be a superpower in the business world, wouldn't it? Pull out your cape and dust it off because we will explore this superpower. We'll break it down and jump into decoding people dynamics.

This chapter is designed to transform the way you do business. Whether winning over clients, inspiring your team, or closing a game-changing deal, understanding the keys of human interaction is necessary for success. We're not just talking theories here. We're talking about science-backed tactics and techniques drawn from psychology and social intelligence. These are the tools that build award-winning teams. They create powerful leaders and sales and marketing strategies that resonate deeply with your audience. Get ready to learn essential techniques to boost your business to seven or eight figures and beyond, and bump your confidence and leadership skills to additional levels. We will cover the secrets of building a lasting rapport, improving your negotiation and communication skills, and mastering your social smarts. Let's turn your understanding of people's dynamics into one of your most valuable business assets. The wisdom and insights you're about to gain are life-changing because you can also use them in other aspects of your life.

Certified as a Six Sigma Greenbelt, I brought dynamic strategies and operational excellence to every venture. But it's not just about what I achieved; it's about how I did it. I'm a competitive dancer. Like a competitive dancer, I've learned to embrace each additional step, adapt to the rhythm, and let the dance of business become second nature. This is the mindset that I bring to you today: a mindset of resilience, innovation, and unwavering commitment to success. In this book, *Dollars & Sense-Abilities for Business Owners*, we'll dive into decoding people dynamics, sometimes known as social smarts, mastering money moves, and creating a culture of success.

You'll learn the strategies that propelled me and hundreds of other clients to soar beyond seven and eight figures. Are you ready to transform your business, break through barriers, and reach heights you never thought possible? This book is your guide to pivoting from challenges to opportunities, from uncertainty to confidence, and from dreaming to achieving. Join me on this transformative journey. Let's unlock the secrets to business success that resonate with who you are and what you stand for. It's time to rise connected and soar beyond your wildest dreams. Are you ready to dance through the challenges and step into your success story? Then, let's begin.

Thank you for taking this first step with me. Remember, we often find significant advantages in the most demanding challenges. This journey is not just about business, it's about your personal growth and success.

The Magic Behind the Million

Imagine for a moment standing at the peak of your business potential. This isn't just a dream; it's your upcoming reality. We will embark on a transformative adventure to decode complex dynamics and primary strategic moves to unlock seven-figure success. Are you ready to turn your entrepreneurial dreams into a reality? Welcome to the pivotal chapter in our book, The Magic Behind the Million Mark.

This milestone, the million-dollar revenue, is more than just a number. It's a testament to a business's viability, sustainability, and potential for growth. It marks the transition from a small, perhaps struggling entity to a stable, flourishing enterprise. Every success story begins with a vision, but what makes it magical? What's the strategy behind it? We will explore how to craft an inspiring and executable vision. But what if you've already hit that million mark? Then, the magic lies in scaling to the elusive eight figures. This leap isn't just about increasing your revenue. It's about deepening your market impact, expanding your influence, and solidifying your legacy in the business world. Success at these levels isn't accidental, it's meticulously designed. We'll explore how to craft a strategy that's not just visionary but actionable. This involves keen foresight, predicting market trends before they become apparent, understanding consumer behavior deeper, and aligning your business model to be reactive and proactive in meeting market demands. Reaching the million or eight-figure mark and beyond is also about adaptation, involving your strategies to stay ahead in a dynamic business landscape, seizing opportunities, and mitigating risks. As we move through this book, remember that whether you're approaching that million mark or aiming for eight figures and beyond, the principles of strategic planning, market foresight, and adaptive business models remain the same. Your journey to these milestones combines ambition, strategic execution, and some entrepreneurial magic.

I will ask you a question you should consider as we move through this chapter. What is your ultimate desire? This isn't just about setting business goals. It's about aligning those goals with your deepest aspirations. Is your desire for financial freedom? The ability to live on your terms, free from monetary constraints? Or is it something different? Is it about making a significant impact, leaving a mark on the world, changing lives, and shaping futures? Or is your desire to create a legacy, building something that outlives you and speaks of your dedication, passion, and vision? It may be a combination of these, and that's okay. This book is more than a guide to business success. It's a pathway to realizing these ultimate desires. By aligning your business strategies with your aspirations, we're not just chasing success. We're creating a life of fulfillment for you. Picture a synergy where each business decision advances your company and brings you closer to your dreams. It's where your professional achievements resonate with your values. We'll explore how to weave your ultimate desires into the fabric of your business. Let's create a blueprint that merges your entrepreneurial journey with your dreams.

This is where your business becomes more than just a venture. It becomes a reflection of your ultimate goals. As we move forward, keep your ultimate desires in your mind. They're the destination of this incredible journey that we're on together. That brings me to your *why*. Welcome to the heart of your entrepreneurial journey. Your why. It's the core of your entire business narrative. Why did you start your business? Was it a passion for innovation? Was it a desire to make an impact? Or the dream of financial independence? This deep-seated motivation is more than just a reason. It's the force that drives you forward, especially when the road gets tough. And it will get tough.

Take a moment to reflect. Think about those early days, that initial spark that set you on this path. Was it to solve a problem you deeply cared about? Was it to fill a gap in the market that you are passionate about? Or was it to create a life that aligns with your values and vision? Understanding your why is understanding the essence of your business's existence. Thinking about it makes you jump out of bed each morning, eager to face the day. You tell your customers that compelling story, building a connection far beyond any transaction. Your why sets you apart in a crowded market. It gives your brand a unique voice and a purpose.

Let me take a moment to share my journey to where I am today. It wasn't just a path. For me, it was a quest to uplift and empower others. Since I began, my goal has been to guide individuals toward their versions of success, whatever that might be for them. From my early days of facing challenges and overcoming obstacles, I realized my true calling lay in inspiring change and fostering growth in others. Every step I've taken in my businesses, every lesson I've learned, has been to equip and empower you. My why is to see you empowered and to help turn your aspirations into achievements. This journey is not just mine. It's ours. My why is present in my organizations. Next Level Connected, for example, allows me to help another business reach its goals or its next level, whether through sales, digital marketing, IT solutions, or business strategy coaching.

Our work model empowers a diverse team to thrive in their careers. We partner with state vocational rehabilitation agencies and other organizations in the community to train and hire individuals with disabilities or situations that benefit from a remote work setup. It's fantastic to provide them with the setup and the tools to be successful in their career journey. In my restaurants, we have a similar work model. I love providing individuals and organizations with solutions or donating to organizations that do beautiful things in our community. How does your why impact your business decisions? It should be the guiding light in your strategic planning and the cornerstone in times of uncertainty. When faced with challenges, recalling your why provides clarity and direction. It's the anchor in the stormy seas of business ownership. There will be stormy seas, so get ready for them. Something else to remember is that your why isn't static. It evolves as you and your business grow. It adapts, strengthening with each success and learning from each setback. Embrace this evolution. Revisit and refine your why regularly, ensuring it resonates with your personal and business growth. Imagine the power of a company driven by a clear, passionate why. It's a business that inspires customer loyalty, fosters a strong company culture, and makes a meaningful impact. Your why isn't just the foundation of your business; it's the magic that can propel it to unimaginable heights. As we move forward in this book, keep your why close. Let it be the lens through which you view every lesson we go through, every strategy, and every piece of advice. There's no limit to where your business can go with your why as your compass.

Now, let's discuss core values. These values are more than words on a website or paper. They're the lifeblood of your enterprise and guide every decision, strategy, and customer interaction. I want you to reflect on what truly drives your business. Is it innovation, pushing the boundaries of what's possible? Community impact, striving to make a tangible difference in people's lives? Or the relentless pursuit of customer satisfaction and exceeding expectations at every turn? Your business values are a strategic compass, directing you through the ever-changing landscape of the business world. They help you stay true to your vision, even when faced with tough choices or unexpected challenges. You will face tough decisions and unforeseen challenges in your business. That's normal; anyone who tells you otherwise has not taken a business to a successful level. How do these values differ from your mission, or why? Think of it this way: your why is your business's heart. It's that emotional core of why you do what you do. Your mission is the brain. That's the practical blueprint of what you aim to achieve. Your values are the soul of your business, shaping its character and defining its path. For instance, if your why is to empower entrepreneurs, your mission might be to provide innovative business solutions. Your values could be innovation, integrity, and empowerment. These values influence how you achieve your mission and color every aspect of your business operations and relationships. They attract like-minded customers, employees, and partners to your business. They're like the magnetic force that aligns your mission with your why. It creates a harmonious and purpose-driven business, which is what you want. It's imperative to take the time to identify and articulate your fundamental business values and embed them into your business practices, brand messaging, and company culture. Remember, decisions become more manageable when your values are clear, and your path to success becomes more apparent. As we continue this journey together, keep those values and your why at the forefront and let them guide you as we explore strategies to catapult your business to new levels. Your values are part of your business and the essence of its success.

We covered your why—your purpose, the heartbeat behind your actions. But let's return to your mission. That's your roadmap, the tangible expression of your why. Let's break that down. First, you'll need to craft a memorable mission statement. Your mission statement needs to be more than just words. It's a promise or a declaration of intent. It should be where your why meets action. We will consider Next Level Connected's mission again, which is dear to my heart. Our mission statement is elevating businesses, empowering communities, and rising connected. It's concise and encapsulates our commitment. Let's review how your why differs from your mission. Remember, your why is the internal driver, and that passion is fueling your journey. The mission, however, is how you execute that passion. It's the what and the how of your aspirations and goals. While your why might be to empower and uplift, your mission is the tangible steps you take to realize that vision. Then, your core values are the pillars of your brand. Are you driven by innovation, quality commitment, or community impact? They guide your business decisions and your customer interactions. For instance, if inclusivity is a value, it should be evident in your hiring practices and corporate culture. Integrate those values into your mission. Your mission should reflect your values. If your value is innovation, your mission might involve pioneering new solutions. It's about aligning what you do with what you believe in.

We're going to take Next Level Connected as an example. Some of our values are inclusion and diversity. We're huge on embracing diversity in our team and client base. We're focused on equipping businesses with the tools and solutions for their success and empowering individuals on our team to advance their career paths, regardless of their challenges. We prioritize purpose over profit and give back as much as we can. We strive to continually offer innovative solutions that will give our clients the edge they need to stay ahead of the competition. We also look for creative ways to accommodate our team members to make them as effective and efficient as possible in their jobs. We remove as much frustration as possible, aiming for a workplace culture everyone wants to be a part of. Remember that a powerful mission statement and clear values don't just guide your business. It also resonates with your customers. They're an essential piece of your brand identity. As you reflect on your mission and values, consider how they manifest in your daily operations. Are they just statements? Or are they living aspects of your business? Craft a mission that's not just something that's pasted up on the website, but an accurate reflection of your ambition.

Let's talk about SMART goals. It's about defining tangible, achievable objectives. Smart goals are Specific, Measurable, Attainable, Relevant, and Time-bound. Each goal should be a clearly defined target. For example, instead of saying, “I want to increase my sales,” a smart goal would be, "I aim to increase sales by 20% in the next quarter." How do we make these goals achievable? Well, we break them down into smaller, actionable steps. Suppose your goal is to grow your customer base by a specific percentage. In that case, we want to start by identifying specific tactics, like improving your website's SEO, launching a social media campaign, or attending various network events. Each of these steps should be measurable. How are you going to track your SEO improvement? What metrics will you use to gauge your social media campaign success? Remember, the relevance of your goals is crucial. Align them with the broader vision of your business. If you want to establish a global brand, each goal you create should be a step toward that vision. Lastly, let's talk about time-bound. Deadlines keep us accountable. They transform dreams and aspirations into action plans.

We've touched on some critical foundations for business success. I hope you're feeling as inspired as I am to take those leaps towards your goals. Next, we'll explore the psychology of success. It's all about getting your mindset geared up for that win.

The Psychology Behind Success

We're about to jump into the psychology of success. Imagine transforming your business dreams into reality. We're not just discussing strategies; we're looking into the mindset secrets that have propelled countless entrepreneurs to phenomenal success.

Before we start, let me share a story about one of my recent clients, Anna. She runs a charming and successful cafe and bakery in the Atlanta area. When we first launched her concept, her major supplier suddenly backed out, and it could have been a total disaster. But together, we saw it as an opportunity. We brainstormed, pivoted, and connected her with a local producer. That shift from that problem transformed her cafe into a community hotspot. We found that connection opened the door to partner with other vendors and suppliers, which would not have been possible had it not been for that minor hiccup. This allowed her to save money and increase her profitability by three times.

I want to touch on some core concepts today. Number one is resilience. Let's consider it your business's immune system. I want to emphasize passion and perseverance when we cover this. It's not just about facing challenges, but owning them.

I'm now going to introduce you to yet another client. His name's Joe, and when his startup faced some funding issues last year, he didn't fold. Instead, he used his passion to pitch to new investors and pivoted his entire business model to get that funding. He eventually secured the funding he needed, and that's resilience in action—using passion to fuel perseverance and turning that potential failure into a steppingstone for success. When you face your next hurdle, ask yourself, how can my passion lead me through this? I have eight organizations that I am the CEO of, so I always have doors closing. When I feel unhappy, I remember this is an opportunity to turn towards something better than I originally planned. Everything happens for a reason. Whether it's life or business, it happens for a reason, and sometimes we won't know why. Sometimes, I'll find that one door closing opened a window that took me further or to a better place strategically than I would have been on had I stayed on that original course. When you're disappointed, get excited. Think about it as being pushed in a better direction than you could have imagined. It's an opportunity to do things differently, in a better way.

Let's move on to the second core point, adaptability. Adaptability has excellent power and leads to success in learning to expect and swiftly adapt to change. This could mean reacting to a new competitor or changing customer preferences in your business. For many of my marketing clients, when social media algorithms change and impact their online store or brand's visibility, I always remind them not to panic. Instead, we adapt by diversifying market strategies, exploring new platforms and new ways of doing things, to connect directly with customers. Adaptability recognizes change and creatively leverages it. Think about your business. What changes are happening around you? How can you adapt creatively? When I'm asked on a podcast or in an interview what I think is the most important skill a business owner possesses, I always have the same answer: adaptability. It can be learned and practiced daily. The ability to become dynamic, to be ready for challenges daily, and to be prepared to pivot at a moment's notice is a skill. It's something that you will find beneficial in running a business. Training your brain to think that way and immediately look for the detour or the workaround. That's how business owners create sustainable and prosperous business models. I expect challenges daily. That helps me to be prepared to pivot.

Let's explore the growth mindset, which involves viewing challenges as growth opportunities. For instance, we'll consider another client, Mark, whom I've worked with for a while. His product launch didn't go as planned. But instead of seeing it as a failure, he saw it as a learning experience. He gathered feedback. He improved the product and did a relaunch. That relaunch was highly successful. That is a growth mindset. He saw setbacks as lessons and opportunities to improve. The next time you face a setback, ask yourself, what can I learn from this? How can this help me grow? How can I do it better next time? I can do it differently by learning from that experience. Consider a challenge in your business or, if you're starting, a challenge in launching your new business. How are you responding? Do you see it as a setback, or d look at it as an opportunity for growth? This reflection is crucial for cultivating a success-oriented mindset. If you want to be successful, train your brain to become dynamic. Train it to prepare for challenges, anticipate them, be ready for them, and be open to learning and pivoting.

To build resilience, you can also start a challenge journal. Note the obstacles daily and then brainstorm creative solutions. For adaptability, we hold a monthly change meeting. We discuss potential market changes and how we plan to adapt. We each set a weekly learning goal to foster a growth mindset within my organization. Identify a new skill or area in your business to improve and work on it daily. For example, we may need to improve our documentation or processes. Read books, learn from other experts, and listen to various perspectives. It's okay to read three books on the same topic. You gain a different perspective every time you read that topic from somebody else or listen to other experts in that field. Teach yourself to learn daily, setting those weekly goals of: I want to know just this little piece, and then I want to implement it.

Next, we'll explore the seven-figure dream from vision to reality. Prepare to turn those dreams into actionable realities. I want you to remember this: Your mindset is your most powerful asset, and within your biggest challenges lie your most significant opportunities. Together, we will unlock these victories, keep pushing, keep growing, be ready to pivot, and stay unstoppable.

Hello, visionaries and go-getters! We're here to turn dreams into reality, laying down the foundation to build something incredible. Ready to bring your seven-figure vision to life? Imagine you're standing atop a mountain, looking out over your business at its peak. This is your seven or eight-figure goal. But getting there requires crystal-clear clarity on who you're serving and how you're different. Think about your ideal, happy customers and what makes them loyal. It's not about being *better* but being different. People connect with something unique, not just superior. Take a moment and picture that pinnacle. What does it look like? Write down who you serve and what sets you apart—this is your differentiating edge. Then, bring that vision to life. Grab a whiteboard or poster and create a vision board. Yes, even if you can't draw! I have one in my office as a daily reminder of where we're headed. Now, let's align your dream with real-world demand. Dive into market research. What do your customers want? What's frustrating them, and how can you solve it? Understand your competitors, spot the gaps, and show why you're the obvious choice. Your offer should be so compelling that they'd be silly to say no. Remember, you're not selling a product—you're selling a result. At Next Level Connected, for example, we don't market "digital marketing services." Instead, we offer a guaranteed spot on Google's first page, with payment only for qualified leads. Why? Because that's what our audience really wants.

For your assignment, create a concise market analysis report. Know your audience's needs and how you can uniquely fulfill them. This is your map through the market landscape.

Lastly, let's pack your toolkit for the journey. Consider everything you need—financial resources, a rockstar team, cutting-edge technology. Make a strategic list, and keep it focused. As we wrap up this up, remember this is just the beginning. You're not just chasing a dream; you're building a future. Next, we'll shatter the myths around seven-figure success and reveal truths to help you get there.

Debunking the 7 Figure Myths

We will slice through the fog of misconceptions to reveal the unfurnished truth about hitting that seven-figure mark and beyond—strap in as we debunk the myths that could hold you back from writing your success story.

Myth number one. The overnight success story. You've seen the headlines and the social media stories. Behind every instant success is a backstory brimming with trial, error, and perseverance. A business explodes onto the scene, riding the viral wave to instant fame. Countless business owners appear to strike gold overnight—an enormous success story. But it's a marathon, not a sprint. Look at me, for example. I've had many obstacles; we will briefly examine my IT company. It started with one client and grew by word of mouth only. No marketing. From zero to seven figures in less than 20 months. Then I ran into obstacles. I didn't have the infrastructure to support what was happening—a thriving division. I never expected it, but then came many overnight jobs, seven days a week and 16 hours a day, because we didn't have the team to support that business. If you look behind that curtain, we struggled to stay on top of things. Frequently, I thought this wasn't for me; then I glanced at my vision board. I reflected on our mission to empower and uplift others and the evolution of all I had dreamed of. Here we are today, more significant than ever expected, with Next Level Connected. We market and provide strategy and growth for other medical practices.

Those stories of overnight sensations rarely mention the grind behind the glamor, that tireless work, and the sheer grit it takes to sustain success and adapt to ever-changing circumstances and markets. After nearly three decades, I've carved out a life where the mountains or the beach beckon. It's a flight away for me, my husband, and my family. Yet, building the structures and automation necessary to do that has been a journey of intense dedication and hard work. Remember that flexibility comes with its own set of responsibilities. There have been plenty of interrupted trips because I'm the linchpin for our team. They count on us, as does the business. When you hear these tales of effortless triumph, take it with a grain of salt. That portrait of success is often cropped tightly, leaving out the vast amount of effort that truly shapes that picture. Success results from hard work and dedication.

Myth number two. Next, we dismantle that *more hours equals more success* fallacy. I just said hard work and dedication lead to success and sustainability. Hard work is sometimes a lot of hours in the beginning. Just because you're burning the midnight oil, it doesn't guarantee a financial breakthrough. People are working many hours, but they're yoked. What creates that breakthrough? Strategic thinking and proven frameworks, solid goals, and plans. Sometimes that takes long hours. We should use those initial long hours to build the right frameworks and put in place the right processes to work smarter, not harder. We want to work more efficiently and effectively. Working too many hours on too many things yourself slows you down and renders your efforts less effective. You're going in too many directions. A tip: Sit down and audit a workday or your week. Identify tasks you could delegate or automate to free up your time. Your time is a resource, and time is money. You should focus on what gets you the most bang for your buck.

Myth number three, moving on to debunk the lone wolf entrepreneur myth. If you think going in alone is the way to seven figures, think again. Collaboration and networking are the silent engines of growth. Let's go back to my client, Emily. Remember her from the last section? It multiplied in value when she partnered with complementary businesses, expanding her reach and resources. This week's tip: Reach out to two business allies. Collaboration can be your force multiplier.

Myth number four. *If you build it, they will come* fantasy. A stellar product isn't enough. Your market needs to know it exists. Effective marketing is critical. I have a client, Alex, who has a fantastic software solution. He brought my team on because it wasn't selling. Everyone on the team thought, how could that solution not sell? We came on, and it gained traction when he started investing as much in marketing as he did in development. People must know it's there. Evaluate your marketing strategy. Are you reaching your ideal customer? Are you meeting them where they are? Are you offering them precisely what they want? Are you selling a result? If you're not selling a result, it's time for a marketing makeover. As we wrap up today's myth journey, it's clear that the road to seven figures is paved with grit, strategy, collaboration, and savvy marketing. Forget about the myths for just a moment and focus on the moves that matter. What stands between you and the seven figures? We will dive into the practical barriers lurking in your path and how you can leap over them. Prepare to tackle this head-on, and we will emerge victorious on the other side. Focus on those tips. Keep challenging the status quo, stay curious, and remember to learn something new each day.

Common Barriers and Their Realities

Have you ever wondered what invisible hurdles might hold you back from that illustrious seven-figure revenue? Let's examine some of the silent obstacles and consider transforming them into launch pads for your success. Are you ready to leap over these hurdles?

The first hurdle, often the comfort zone, is a familiar and cozy place. However, it's also where growth takes a back seat. Remaining within this zone means you're missing out on the exhilarating ride of success. It's not the lack of opportunities but the *resistance to change* that creates this barrier. Imagine this: You've found a comfortable pace in your business. It's tempting to stay here, but comfort is often the first sign of an upcoming plateau. By stepping out of this zone, you avoid stagnation and open the door to new opportunities and growth. Think of it like running on a treadmill. You're moving, but not forward. I had a client; his tavern was one of the town's favorites. It was doing okay, but it also hit that plateau. He wasn't seeing growth. We sat down, revamped his menu, and changed the ambiance. We shattered through the seven-figure ceiling with him. The tip to shattering this invisible wall is to introduce one innovation this quarter in your business, whether it's a new product line, a fresh marketing tactic, or disrupting your routine to spark growth. Embrace change, challenge the status quo, and identify just one aspect of your business that's been comfortable for too long. Let's strategize to innovate. Another thing that often stands in the way—this is big—is the fear of scaling. You're thinking, *Christy, what are you talking about? I'm looking to scale. I'm not afraid of that.* If we look down inside, sometimes the thought of scaling looms large. It can cast a What if? What if I lose my company culture? What if I can't keep up with the pace? What if this strategy doesn't work? This fear can keep your business in a perpetual state of smallness, stifling its true potential. We can conquer this fear by scaling intelligent strategies. Focus on what scaling means for your business. Is it more staff, larger premises, or a broader market reach? Then, you take a calculated step toward one of those areas. When you feel yourself questioning, what if it won't work? Instead, I say, "But what if it does work?" Then, I envision what that looks like for me.

The third barrier we face is the delegation dilemma. Delegating isn't just about offloading tasks. It's about empowering others to take the reins where it's appropriate. That's the key. The hurdle here is not the act of delegation, but the *reluctance to trust others* with your vision. I have had to practice this over the years. It's been a struggle for me. I overcame this by practicing strategic delegation. I start with less critical tasks, and as trust builds in the employee, the vendor, or the contractor, I hand over more significant responsibilities. This not only clears my plate but prepares my business for scalable success. Strategic delegation is not just about getting things off your plate, but about empowering others and preparing your business for growth. As we break down these barriers together, remember that the path to seven figures will be paved with persistence and smart moves. Delegating is one of those. Until our next breakthrough, remember the only limits that exist are the ones that you place on yourself. Dare to leap over these hurdles, and you'll find your business soaring to heights you only once imagined.

External Hurdles vs. Internal Battles

Imagine you're behind the wheel. The highway's your market landscape. Now, picture traffic jams, detours, and roadblocks. These are the external hurdles that test your patience and your schedule. In the driver's seat, your hands tight on that wheel, is your determination, which is the fuel against the doubts, whispering you might never reach your destination. That whisper, those doubts, those are your internal battles. Now, we gear up to navigate through these challenges, converting red lights into green ones and using every bump in the road to build momentum toward your goals. External hurdles are like changing weather patterns. They're market shifts, regulatory updates, competition surges, and other events. They're beyond our control, yet we can prepare for them. Just like we can watch the sky for an incoming storm that impacts our outdoor plans for the day, a savvy business leader can anticipate market trends. One of the biggest things you can do is to stay informed. Keep a market weather station, if you will, a dashboard where you track industry changes, consumer behavior, and your competitor's movements. What are they up to? This isn't paranoia; it's preparation. When the market shifts, you'll be the first to reveal your newest plans and adjust your climb.

Now, let's turn inward to our internal battles. These are the doubts, fears, those limiting beliefs, the whispers: turn back, it's too tough ahead, and you can't do it. Yet it's within these internal echoes that we find our inner strength. Just as the mind commands the body to perform an action or move yourself forward, your willpower commands your business to soar. Develop a mindset about them. This is where you identify negative patterns and actively work to replace them with affirmations of your capability and vision. The self-dialogue rewrite isn't just a little motivational talk; it's the actual reprogramming of the very core of your business owner drive that's in your mind. Much of what we've explored in this section might feel like we focus heavily on mindset coaching. Well, you're right; that's what we're doing. I always start here with these foundational principles for a fundamental reason.

These principles are the driving force behind everything we will dive into next. That will be the practical strategies, frameworks, and actionable tips. What we've learned so far, the lessons, the insights, and what we've been talking about, are the bedrock of your success. Think of it as laying down the essential groundwork before you build a house. Now that we've got our foundation solid and ready, it's time to roll up our sleeves and start constructing your business. We're about to shift gears from mindset to action.

The upcoming chapters are packed with directions, plans, and hands-on tools to transform your business goals into tangible achievements. Buckle up because we are just starting, and the best is yet to come. As we wrap up this chapter, let's review it. Remember that life will throw curve balls like our external hurdles. They keep changing and can surprise you when you least expect it. But guess what? They're no match for a mind that's set and ready. Then there are the internal fights, the doubts, and what ifs. They're tough, but they can't silence that deep down voice that says, I've got this, or what if it works? What if I am successful?

Looking ahead to our next chapter, Embracing Challenges, The Dynamic Approach. We will take all of this we've learned and make it benefit us. Think of it as turning every setback into a step up, every challenge into a chance to shine. We're going to learn how to dance right through those difficulties. This was the foundation. Keep aiming high and remember that you're not just building a company; you're creating your own success story—every moment, every action, including reading this book. Stay strong, stay faithful, and always keep pushing forward.

Chapter 2 Decisiveness-Making Choices that Fuel Growth

We're diving into the heart of decisiveness, that art of making choices that don't just keep your business afloat but propel it to new heights. Are you ready to make choices that will ignite growth in your business?

First, let's picture us standing at a crossroads. One path is the path of your comfort zone. It's familiar. The other is less traveled and filled with unknowns but brimming with potential. The decision you make here can redefine your business story. Think about the last major decision you made for your business. How did it feel? Were you feeling that weight of uncertainty? Were you feeling a buzz of possibility? Decisiveness isn't just about making choices; it's about making informed choices that drive your business forward, and here's how we do that. We start with clarity—understanding your business goals. Then, you gather intel, data, trends, customer feedback, etc. The more data you have, the better. Next, we weigh the risks but do it without letting fear be our compass. The most significant periods of success or results I've seen in my businesses always came from stepping outside of my comfort zone. *Growth cannot occur when you're comfortable.* I advise clients to *label the uncomfortable feeling* as their *growth feeling* each time it hits. This re-trains your brain to view it as exciting-growth!

When it comes to making bold business moves, I rely on the DECIDE framework: Define, Explore, Create, Implement, Drive, and Evaluate. This isn't just a strategy; it's a way to navigate decisions with confidence.

Define your goal. Start by getting crystal clear on what you want to achieve. Are you aiming to boost sales, launch a new product, or improve customer service? A well-defined, specific goal will serve as your anchor throughout the decision-making process. For example, you might aim to increase sales by 20% in Q4—clear, specific, and measurable.

Explore your options. Gather information and perspectives. Consult with experts and mentors, attend webinars, or join mastermind groups. Every new insight sharpens your perspective, helping you weigh different approaches and uncover solutions.

Create a detailed plan. With your goal set and options explored, develop a specific action plan. Outline the steps, timelines, resources, and potential risks. Planning isn't about just aiming for the goal; it's about foreseeing challenges and setting a roadmap to overcome them.

Implement your plan. This is where the rubber meets the road. Execution demands focus and commitment. Stay adaptable and ready to adjust as needed—remember, even the best plan is only as effective as its execution.

Drive the plan forward. Whether it's motivating your team or yourself, actively manage and lead the process. Keep monitoring progress and remain dedicated to your goal. Confidence and commitment are key to pushing through.

Evaluate the outcome. After each step, take time to assess what worked and what didn't. Each project, plan, and decision offers valuable insights that inform your next steps. Continual evaluation drives growth, letting you refine and improve with every effort.

The DECIDE framework is more than a checklist; it's a mindset that fosters proactive and thoughtful decision-making. Mastering it will help you approach business decisions with greater clarity and purpose. As we wrap up, remember that decisiveness is your superpower in business. Your choices define your path. By using this framework, you can make bold, growth-focused decisions with confidence. Next, we'll dive into the importance of calculated risks and how they can unlock new opportunities. So, keep making those strategic choices, and watch your business soar.

Calculated Risks in Action

We're going to cover calculated risks in action. Have you ever stood at the edge of a new venture and felt both exhilaration and apprehension? We will step into that space where your bold moves meet strategic planning. Taking risks in business can feel like walking on a tightrope, but it shouldn't. It's all about calculated risks, combining the courage to step forward with the wisdom to know where you're stepping. First, what is a calculated risk? It's a risk that's been carefully evaluated. That means you already know the potential downsides and contemplated the gains. They can be huge gains for your business, but it's important to remember that this is not about taking reckless leaps into the unknown. It's about informed strategic moves that push your business forward.

We're going to break it down and use the R.I.S.K. framework today. R.I.S.K. stands for Research, Intuition, Strategy, and Knowledge. Let's take it to the whiteboard because, for me, it's all about writing it out. If you want to write it down on paper, that's great. In wrapping up, remember that every business success story has risks. The beauty of calculated risks is that they're grounded in thoughtfulness and planning.

Speaking of daring, our next session, Escaping Paralysis: Overcoming Fear of Wrong Choices, will take us even deeper into mastering the art of decisive action without fear holding you back.

Escaping Analysis Paralysis and Tackling Fear in Decision-Making

We've all been there—frozen at the crossroads, wondering if we're about to make a mistake. It's that moment of doubt that can hold you back. But let's face it: how you handle these moments sets you apart. Fear of making the wrong choice can paralyze you, but it doesn't have to. Here's how to shake off that analysis paralysis and step forward confidently:

Acknowledge the Fear: It's natural to feel scared. But it's how you respond to fear that counts. Fear is a signal, not a stop sign.

Redefine Failure: View each decision as a learning opportunity. The most successful stories are full of lessons from missteps. Every mistake I've made has taught me something invaluable.

Take Small Steps: Start with minor decisions to build your confidence. Each small success is a steppingstone, strengthening your ability to tackle larger challenges.

Seek Fresh Perspectives: A new viewpoint can be the key to moving forward. Talk to mentors, peers, or even clients to gain clarity. Learning from others' experiences is powerful. I'm sharing my lessons with you here, so take advantage and learn from them.

Imagine deciding without fear, knowing that each choice fuels your business growth. That's the goal. Embrace your challenges, learn from mistakes, and let them drive you forward. We make over 35,000 small decisions daily—what to eat, whether to grab a drink. Our brains handle countless choices, big and small. It's easy to let fear of a wrong move slow us down. Sometimes, we wait too long, and the opportunity passes. Quick decisions are crucial, especially when running a business.

Let me share a quick story. One night at one of my restaurants, a pipe burst. Water was everywhere, and I had to decide fast: stay open, shut down, call a plumber? With a team on-site, we acted quickly. Business often demands these quick choices: which tool to buy, what offer to make, how to respond on the spot. Practice making small decisions swiftly and analyzing your data fast. Even ordering lunch—skim the menu, choose quickly, and move on. Confidence in decision-making is built through practice. You won't always make the right choice, and that's okay. It's unrealistic to expect perfection. Feel the paralysis? It's normal, especially when the stakes are high. But with the strategies we're discussing, you can navigate decisions with confidence. As we continue, we'll delve into a tool that turns uncertainty into a structured process—the Decision-Making Matrix. It's about making bold moves with a safety net of strategy. Let's tackle those decisions and pave the way for your business to thrive.

The Decision-Making Matrix

We're going to dive into decision-making again and focus on the decision-making matrix. Decision-making in business can feel like navigating a very complex maze. We will help you turn those tough decisions into steppingstones for success. Imagine that you're standing at a crossroads and each path represents a different business decision. Some paths can look clear. Sometimes, there's a bit of fog on the path, and you can't see down there. This is where your decision-making matrix will come into play. The matrix is a straightforward framework tool I use. It's all about assessing two key factors: impact and urgency. Ask yourself, how much impact will this decision have on my business? Number two, how urgent is it? This approach transforms overwhelming choices into manageable ones. By placing these decisions inside the decision matrix, you can look at them and see which ones demand immediate attention and which ones can be planned for later. First, look at categorizing those decisions based on their impact, high impact, and low impact. Then, determine its urgency. What type of priority level are we looking at here? This process will help you prioritize your actions and ensure that you focus on what truly matters for your business growth.

In our next section, Expecting the Unexpected Embracing Change, we prepare for the unforeseen. We'll discuss how to gracefully navigate the inevitable changes and surprises that come into the business world.

Expecting the Unexpected

Business, like weather, is ever-changing. But instead of fearing it, let's turn those changes into our advantage. I want to share a quick story about my restaurants. When the pandemic hit, everything changed overnight. Our suburban location, known for its ambiance and in-house dining experience, had to close its doors. Instead of seeing this as a setback, we pivoted to online ordering and expanded our delivery options. We set up more pickup spaces, retrained our staff for outdoor dining, and even kept some of these innovations after reopening. Now, delivery adds about 10% to our monthly revenue. Embracing change opened a new revenue stream for us. This experience taught me that adapting quickly is crucial. Staying updated on industry trends, as we do at Next Level Connected, keeps us ahead. We host brainstorming sessions to tap into our team's ideas, constantly adapting to market feedback. Flexibility in your business plan is essential—don't be afraid to tweak strategies or even do an overhaul if needed. Cultivating an agile mindset isn't just about following trends; it's about fostering a culture of continuous learning. Encourage your team to share new ideas and reward innovation. A team that's equipped to handle change becomes your strongest asset when it's time to pivot. Remember, change is inevitable;

it's your response to it that shapes your success. Take challenges as steppingstones for growth. Just like resistance strengthens your muscles, challenges sharpen problem-solving skills. They spark creativity and can lead to innovations you hadn't even considered. When you face a challenge, it's not the obstacle itself but how you respond that matters. Reframing challenges into growth opportunities is powerful. Use tools like the SWOT analysis to navigate these changes effectively. At Next Level Connected, our strengths include offering unique, holistic services. But we were also a new player in the competitive IT and digital marketing space, facing limited market reach and brand recognition. By identifying these weaknesses, we could address them strategically, leveraging emerging tech like AI for advanced marketing services. Our nimble size allowed us to deliver personalized services that big businesses couldn't match.

The ability to pivot is key. In business, like on a mountain trail, sometimes you have to change your route due to unexpected obstacles. Pivoting means adjusting your plan, evaluating what's working, and identifying new market opportunities. It may involve reallocating resources, retraining your team, or investing in new technology. Seeking feedback from both customers and employees can provide invaluable insights and ensure you're ready for the next shift. Take one of my e-commerce clients as an example. Initially, they were a brick-and-mortar store. Facing stiff competition, we re-evaluated their strategy, focusing on e-commerce and reducing their physical footprint. Their store became a fulfillment center, cutting costs and boosting efficiency. Today, 75% of their sales are online, and their revenue has tripled. This was only possible because they were open to change and willing to pivot. When it comes to anticipating change, think like a weather forecaster. Analyze market trends, listen to your customers, and monitor competitors. Even if predictions aren't always perfect, they can prepare you to adapt when the unexpected happens. The best approach is to stay ready and foster a mindset that sees change as an opportunity rather than a threat. As you incorporate this outlook, you'll find that what once seemed like an obstacle can become a steppingstone to greater success.

Adaptability is key in today's fast-paced business world, and I use the A-D-A-P-T framework to guide my decisions. Here's how it breaks down:

A: Assess – Start by evaluating where your business stands. What's working? What isn't? This is where the SWOT analysis comes in handy. Identify strengths, weaknesses, opportunities, and threats.

D: Develop – Based on your assessment, craft strategies to address the gaps. It could mean diversifying products, ramping up marketing, or adjusting your advertising methods. Think of it as analyzing the weather: read the conditions and plan your approach accordingly.

A: Action – This is where strategy meets execution. Action is what separates successful businesses from those stuck in perpetual planning. I worked with a medical practice that was great at identifying issues and brainstorming solutions but struggled with follow-through. Remember, even the best strategy is pointless without execution.

P: Progress – Monitor your progress constantly. Ask yourself: Are you moving toward your goal? What's the data telling you? Is your strategy working, or do you need to pivot? Don't make the mistake of overlooking progress tracking—it's your feedback loop for success.

T: Transform – Be ready to evolve beyond current market needs. Cultivate a growth mindset not just for yourself but throughout your team. Instill this attitude in your team right from onboarding. Create a culture where adaptability is second nature.

Resilience should be a part of your business DNA. Encourage team members to share ideas, even if they're not fully formed. You don't need the whole plan to start a discussion. This openness can lead to breakthroughs when team members brainstorm together, combining their strengths. Inspire an adaptive culture through continuous training and open communication. Make change exciting rather than daunting. Just like when I start a new dance season, the choreography can feel challenging initially. But once I break it down and practice, it all falls into place beautifully. Apply that same muscle memory to your business: continually assess, improve, and thrive. Adaptability is about being proactive rather than reactive. It's not just about keeping up—it's about positioning yourself to move ahead. Business leaders who embrace this mindset soar to seven, eight, and even nine figures by being swift and adaptable. Make adaptability a part of your core, and watch your business evolve with purpose.

Adaptation Short Bonus

Funny story I wanted to share with everyone today about adaptation. I went in for this volunteer presentation with a group of high school students, and the goal was to discuss how to find your passion, your career, and how to choose your future path. I have spoken to this group once before, so they know me, and I'm about five minutes in, and I found with this group, or this age group specifically, it's a great idea to engage the audience a few minutes in, really open up the Q&A so that I can tailor the rest of my approach to different questions and things I see in the chat. I open the Q&A box, and I ask for questions. I want you to guess what the most asked question was in that chat box. It was, "Hey, Miss Christy, what shoes are you wearing today? Do they have sparkles? Are they heels? What color are they? Can we see them?" What do I do? I show off my shoes and let them know that, yeah, absolutely, of course, they're heels. No, they don't have sparkles, but they do have fabulous enormous bows. What it allowed me to do, though, was immediately adapt my presentation and segue into the piece on authenticity and how important it is to use your uniqueness in your career and life. Use that as a strike to build confidence in everything you do and really be able to move forward with passion. It turned out to be a really engaging presentation. When you're doing presentations, when you are in public speaking, it's important to adapt your approach and the way you deliver the rest of your information based on the audience's reactions. I thought it was funny that one of my most impactful presentations for this high school group happened because of questions on shoes.

Pivoting from Panic to Solutions Bonus

Ever had technology betray you at the worst possible moment? Well, I had a client call today. They said, "I was projecting my presentation to the podcast room screen, and it failed. Panic ensued." I, of course, guided them through fixing the issue and re-recording. But this reminded me that life is 10% what happens and 90% how you respond. Anytime life tosses you a mishap or a challenge, stop and ask yourself, *are you reacting or are you responding?* Because one's impulsive and one's strategic. Want a successful career and less stress and anxiety in life? Then practice transforming panic into a plan. Remind yourself in these situations, *how can I respond that results in a solution*? It will help you avoid that loss of control feeling and help you quickly, confidently handle the situation. Master this and you'll not only shine in meetings, but in life.

Be Ready to Pivot Short Bonus Reminder

You may not want to hear this, but if you're like me, your attempt at making everything perfect is holding you back from success. My biggest business regret is that I didn't launch my first business sooner. Are you launching a business, a new service, or product, or even just content? Don't get stuck perfecting everything before you start. Here's my advice. Step one, launch. Don't wait for everything to be perfect. Get your product or service to the market quickly. Why? Because that's where you'll learn the most. Collect feedback from real customers and use that data to make improvements. Second, embrace feedback and be ready to pivot. It's all about continuous improvement. Be willing to change your approach based on what you learn. It's okay to adjust your course along the way. Expect that you won't need to. The goal is to find a sustainable business model. You may not have it all figured out in the beginning and that's okay. Remember that. Keep testing, learning, and adapting. That's the key to success. Before launching your business, or even if you're already up and running, remember to launch quickly, embrace feedback, and be ready to pivot.

The Power of Yet Short Bonus

You told yourself you can't do it. Wait for it. I was really struggling this week with meeting my book deadlines and I was feeling overwhelmed, and I said the words *I can't* when describing things to my husband.

I can't—*yet*. I printed this and hung it in my office. The words *I can't* come out of your mouth, and this is where most of us stop, but what if you add the tiny word *yet*? It changes everything. Adding yet turns doubt into a journey, a mission, a goal. It's not about whether you can or can't, it's about when.

Next time you think I can't, slap a yet on it and then think about what it would take to say I can, or I have because mindset, I promise, it's everything.

Budget Your Business Worksheet-Simple Steps to Financial Clarity

Struggling to keep track of your business finances? This simplistic monthly budgeting tracker is designed just for you. With this simple, user-friendly worksheet, you can easily monitor your sales, expenses, and profits each month. Gain financial clarity and make smarter decisions to keep your business on the right track. Start budgeting like a pro today!

http://bit.ly/3Xi38tO

Chapter 3 Mastering Money Management

Understanding your finances isn't optional—it's essential for business success. Many clients tell me, "Christy, I have a finance team or a CPA, so I don't need to worry about it." While you don't have to be a finance expert, having a grasp of the basics is crucial. Knowing the financial fundamentals helps you budget, align resources, and make informed decisions for scaling your business. I've worked with countless clients, diving into their financials to cut costs and boost profits. Even though I focus on growth, I know that understanding cash flow, profit and loss, and budgeting is the foundation. Budgeting and financial planning are not just about today; they're about preparing for tomorrow, next year, and beyond. To hit seven or eight figures, your financial plan must support your goals. It's about looking at where you want to be, not just what's happening now. Proactively setting aside funds for future opportunities and unexpected challenges is essential.

Take my Atlanta Bread restaurant, for example. We have a fund called *It Broke* because, well, things break. Last summer, two AC units gave out within six weeks. Because we had that fund, we could make repairs without hesitation. You never know when a sudden opportunity might pop up, like the time we were approved to provide cybersecurity training to law firms. By having a fund ready, we quickly invested in this new stream of revenue and seized the chance. Allocate resources where they'll give you the highest ROI. Use tools like SWOT analysis and decision matrices to identify and invest in areas like technology, talent, or marketing. For example, at Next Level Connected, we initially offered only IT support. As we identified client needs, we added business strategy, marketing, and sales services, creating a one-stop shop. This not only opened multiple revenue streams but also strengthened long-term client relationships. Ultimately, scaling your business requires strategic investments and the ability to adapt. The frameworks I'm sharing with you helped us hit seven figures in under 20 months, and we're on track for eight figures within three years. I've used these strategies with thousands of clients, guiding them to achieve their growth goals. Remember, mastering money management is the key to building a thriving business.

Key Lessons for Growth

Reallocate Resources Wisely: Always be prepared to reallocate funds where needed to seize growth opportunities. Flexibility is crucial in adjusting to business needs.

Regular Budget Reviews: Schedule regular budget reviews—monthly, quarterly, or bi-annually. Assess how your resources are allocated and make necessary adjustments based on current needs. This is something I learned the hard way, and you can avoid mistakes by staying proactive.

Adaptability is Key: Your budget should be dynamic, not set in stone. Regularly review and adjust it to meet your business's evolving needs.

Learning from failures—especially others'—is invaluable. Keep your budget flexible, regularly assess your progress, and reallocate where needed to fuel your business growth.

One lesson I learned the hard way: I wasn't meeting with my finance team regularly to drill down into our profit-and-loss (P&L) statements. As a business owner, I strongly recommend reviewing your P&Ls consistently—whether you use QuickBooks, a CPA, or other software. Don't just focus on the bottom line; dig deeper into what drives those profits and losses. Even if your numbers are positive, take time to analyze them. You may find opportunities to increase revenue or avoid missed chances to maximize profits. Regular budget reviews are essential. Don't leave them entirely in someone else's hands. Adjust your budget mid-year or mid-month if needed, based on any opportunities or issues that arise. Your budget should be flexible and responsive. I made the mistake of not reviewing my restaurant's P&Ls closely. Six months in, I realized we were less profitable than last year. After investigating, I found we hadn't adjusted our prices in line with rising food costs. Though we were on track for the budget, we missed out on extra profits. Learn from my mistake—monitor closely even when a team is watching the budget. You need to understand your budget and P&L statements and tailor them to your company's needs. Financial strategy is an ongoing process of review, refinement, and adjustment. Even if you're not managing every detail, force yourself to learn. Staying connected to your business's evolving financial needs is crucial. Cash flow is the lifeblood of your business, just like the rhythm in a well-choreographed dance. It's about ensuring that your inflows and outflows are perfectly synchronized. Positive cash flow isn't just numbers on a spreadsheet; it's a sign of your business's vitality and agility. Managing cash flow means balancing the money coming in (inflows) and going out (outflows) to ensure you have enough on hand to cover obligations like payroll and overhead.

Here are key strategies to maintain positive cash flow:

Invoice promptly and follow up–Just like timing in a dance, timing in invoicing is crucial. Send invoices promptly and track payments to avoid delayed cash inflow. Early in my business, I neglected this, causing cash flow issues that required a short-term loan to cover expenses. Avoid this by using project tracking software or spreadsheets to stay on top of invoicing.

Manage expenditures–Cut back on non-essential expenses. Small monthly fees can add up. Regularly review your expenses, analyze whether they are necessary, and reduce or eliminate unnecessary costs. Negotiate with suppliers and vendors for better rates—it can save you money over time.

Maintain a cash reserve–Having a financial safety net is crucial for unexpected expenses or opportunities. Aim to keep a 20% cash reserve for each business division. Seasonal fluctuations, common in many businesses, require adjustments like offering subscription-based services for steadier cash flow. Regularly review your budget to stay ahead of cash flow challenges. Cash flow management is about maintaining stability while allowing for growth. Frequent reviews, whether weekly or monthly, are essential to ensure you're always on top of your financial health. By implementing these strategies, you'll ensure your business is set up for sustained revenue and growth.

Next, we'll dive into cost management, focusing on spending wisely and saving smartly.

Cash Management

Cash management is crucial for scaling your business and freeing up resources for growth. Start by analyzing every expense. Ask, "Is this bringing value to my business?" Cutting unnecessary costs allows you to allocate funds toward expansion. You need to review your credit card and bank statements, P&Ls, and categorize costs as essential or non-essential. I recommend using software like QuickBooks for expense tracking, which simplifies the process and helps you identify savings opportunities. For example, when reviewing expenses at Next Level Connected, I found we were overspending on underutilized software. Canceling those subscriptions allowed us to reallocate funds to enhance customer services. Even small monthly fees add up. I saved $5,000 annually for a client by consolidating software subscriptions, then reinvested that into marketing, which returned $20,000. Always evaluate whether each cost is necessary and brings value to your business, whether directly or indirectly (like training). Cutting unnecessary costs doesn't mean sacrificing quality, but being resourceful. Regularly assess vendor contracts, negotiate better terms, and explore cost-effective alternatives. When savings are realized, reinvest them into profitable ventures like marketing or R&D to accelerate growth. By doing this, you can scale faster, diversify revenue streams, and ensure you're putting funds toward areas that drive growth. Reinvesting strategically, especially early on, can help you break through to seven figures. Once you hit key milestones, you can set aside profits, but initially, focus on reinvesting savings to maximize your growth potential.

To help your business grow, diversifying investments is key. Don't put all your eggs in one basket—spread your investments across multiple areas to mitigate risks. Relying on one contract or income stream can be dangerous, especially if economic changes affect that area. Diversify by setting up multiple streams of income, even within the same niche. For example, if you're a fitness coach, you can offer one-on-one coaching, group coaching, courses, speaking engagements, and partnerships with vendors for supplements. This creates a more secure and resilient income flow. Long-term investments are like planting a tree—nurture them, and they will provide returns for a lifetime. Although they may take time to grow, focus on investments that promise long-term stability and returns, besides scaling faster through reinvesting in marketing.

Leverage technology to grow your business, no matter your industry. Even if your business is niche, like reupholstery services, technology can streamline processes, analyze data, and expand your reach. For example, by building a website, utilizing social media for organic growth, and running ads, we helped a reupholstery business increase its revenue by over 200%. Technology is no longer optional—it's necessary for expansion and staying competitive. Even if technology isn't central to your fieldwork, leveraging it is essential to gaining a competitive edge and opening additional revenue streams. Think of your investment portfolio like an art collection—diversity adds depth and resilience. Diversifying your investments across asset classes, industries, and geographical locations helps mitigate risks and ensures your business can withstand economic fluctuations. Regularly assess market trends and adjust your investments to remain aligned with market conditions. This approach allows you to scale quickly and make smarter financial decisions.

When evaluating financial decisions, use a decision matrix to guide you. Take control of your finances—even with a team in place, understand your P&Ls, the financial implications of your strategies, and how to reallocate resources for the best return on investment. Applying these tips will help you transform your financial goals into tangible successes.

We'll soon dive into understanding human behavior and how to leverage it for business growth. Until then, keep mastering, growing, and working toward your goals.

Chapter 4
Decoding People Dynamics

I want you to start by imagining yourself walking into a room and instantly being able to connect with everyone you meet. Picture yourself navigating complex negotiations with ease and understanding exactly what drives the person sitting across from you. This skill would be a superpower in the world of business, wouldn't it? Well, pull out your cape and dust it off, because today we're going to go through this superpower. We're going to break it down.

We're going to jump into decoding people dynamics. It's a chapter designed to transform the way you do business, whether it's winning over clients, inspiring your team or closing a game changing deal, understanding the keys of human interaction is necessary for success. We're not just talking theories here. We're talking about science, fact, tactics, and techniques that are drawn from psychology and social intelligence. These are the tools that award-winning teams used to create powerful leaders, and they create sales and marketing strategies that resonate deeply with your audience. Get ready to learn techniques that will be important in boosting your business, but also to bump your confidence and leadership skills. We're going to talk about the secrets of building a lasting rapport, improving negotiation and communication skills, and mastering your social smarts, the sixth sense. Let's turn your understanding of people's dynamics into one of your most valuable business assets. The wisdom and insights that you're about to gain are life changing because you can also use them in other aspects of your life.

The Charisma Factor Becoming Irresistibly Likable

Let's start by understanding what charisma is. Charisma is the ability to attract, charm, and influence the people around you. It's often seen as a combination of confidence, warmth, and authenticity. We know those people where it's like a magnet is pulling us in. It's who we want to be around. It's exactly who we want to lead. Who do we want to take over this presentation? Who do we want to go hang out with at this party? What group do we want to be in? We all know that person. They have something that attracts everybody. They're extremely likable, fun, and positive. They inspire and motivate. I know a lot of us sitting here you are saying, "That's not me. I wish it was. I just wasn't born with that personality trait." I want you to remember this. If you remember nothing else, charisma is not a personality trait. That magnetic personality, having charisma, being able to attract everybody to you, it's not something you're born with. It is a practiced skill. It is not something that you're born with. That's good news for most of us. For me, it's good news. I can practice being that person. We're going to talk about some of the key components to becoming that magnetic personality in the room, that magnet attracting everybody's attention.

Key components of charisma, number one, is confidence. *I wasn't born with confidence. I see those people. They're just confident in everything they do. They can get up on stage. They don't get nervous. They can speak to a group of people. They know what they're talking about.* The more you practice it, the more it becomes natural. Suddenly, that is who you are. It's buried in each of us. It is activated with practice. Confidence is showing belief in yourself and conveying that belief to others. We're going to go over that one. Empathy is the ability to understand and share the feelings of others. Create that deep connection with empathy, that understanding. Expressiveness, communicating effectively. That is a key component of charisma. Then finally, authenticity. Being genuine to be oneself. It builds trust and rapport. *How can I be authentic and have confidence?* Again, practice. They are all buried inside you, and you just refine them. You bring them out and activate them. You have a side of you that is confident. It's a skill you practice. Your confident self is a choice. *I don't have what all these other people have.* Confidence is a choice. It's before you walk into that presentation, work, the room at a party, or at an event. At a keynote speaking experience, it's making a choice to display a certain set of behaviors. That's all confidence is. The more you practice it, the more it becomes natural, and you refine that natural skill. I travel around and I teach people how to speak confidently, how to speak and present effectively on stage, how to be confident and own the room. I can train anybody on that, but I can't train you on your authentic self. I can help you determine what that is, who that is based on your experiences, how you feel about things, how you react to things, but who you are, dig down deep into what's special about you. What makes you different?

For example, I have a medical condition called a gamma globulinemia. I was born with it. It's a big fancy term for, I don't make the proteins that activate my immune system. We've all seen the show or the movie the boy in the bubble. I was born with that immune deficiency. My genes are broken. They don't produce what I need. That's something unique to me. For the longest time, I hid that in my career, in my positions. I thought this was a weakness. I just wanted to be normal. What I found was the experience I gained from those treatments, the way it shaped everything I did, the drive to become a health advocate in my spare time, to really work in areas where I was helping others overcome challenges from a medical condition, a disability, an accident, that has changed the trajectory of their career. I developed a program within our organizations that partner with vocational rehabilitation and helps to train individuals to do something different, better, sometimes something that they can be successful in and continue their career. They might've had their career derailed, but we're able to put it on a different track and shoot it back uphill again and grow their career, give them a fantastic opportunity to bring everything they are, all that experience with them, how to overcome the challenges, and accommodate some of those more challenging aspects of their condition. How can we leverage that? How can we work around that? How can we make it a part of what they do? I would not have that drive. That would not be me if I didn't have what I have. Another thing people tell me, "Oh, Christy, I can't make eye contact. I can't speak. I can't do whatever it is. I can't be confident."

Did you know that part of my condition also causes my body to attack itself in other areas? One of those areas I have misshaped eyelids, they droop. My eyelids turn in and I have thousands of eyelashes that lay on my eye or poke my eye. I pluck my eyes two, three times a day or whenever it's needed. I go in every two weeks and have my eye doctor remove the rest. I have no eyelashes. I have to either fake them on or draw on to deter from me not having them. Growing up, that was a challenge for me. I felt very unconfident when people saw me dabbing my eyes because they water constantly, because my tear duct is closed and does not drain. It's watering, but there's nowhere for the water to go. I was always so self-conscious. I thought I can't get up on stage and speak to thousands if I have a tissue in my hand and I'm dabbing my eye. But guess what? I've turned it into a part of my presentations, using my experience to help others overcome their own unique challenges. I have made that a part of me. It's who I am. I bring all of that into my presentations, trainings, mission, and my goal.

Be your authentic self while still refining skills and behaviors such as confidence, empathy, things that you're saying, that's not naturally me. It's not natural for anybody. You are shaped by whatever you heard around you, the communication you grew up with, the environment you grew up in shaped the way you show confidence or the behaviors you use that determine is that confident or not, is that empathetic or not? The same way you are shaped, you can shape or train yourself to behave however you'd like. Be whoever you want to be. That's the secret. Get rid of the thought that's just not you. Find what truly makes you authentic. What is your differentiating edge? Weave that into all those newfound skills that we're going to go over. Let's start with how to become more confident. How do we appear more confident? Body language is big. Body language, posture, sit tall, stand tall. I like to stand when I speak. It is hard for me to sit down. You see me bouncing around, moving body language. Keep your head high when you're walking. Next time you're just walking through the store or you're walking outside or you're walking into a room, I want you to practice looking straight out at everyone. You don't have to focus on one person if you're feeling uncomfortable, but practice on keeping your head up and eyes out. Not only are you going to appear more confident to everybody else, but you will feel more confident. It's proven. Test it. It works. Posture. When you're standing tall, when your shoulders are back, that good posture exudes confidence. I know it sounds crazy, but you will feel more confident, too. It is in your brain. It will boost that level of confidence when your posture is that of confident posture.

I struggle with eye contact. I sometimes have trouble looking out at the light. I'm extremely photosensitive because of my eyes. I dab my eyes a lot. I don't explain myself. If somebody asks, I'm happy to let them know. But I do not justify it. That's another big one with confidence. Don't justify and don't validate. When you're giving excuses or you're justifying without the question being asked, it comes across as trying to over-explain yourself and a very unconfident behavior. Be OK with who you are. It does not detract from the value of the message that I'm bringing or from my desire to help others in the audience. Maintain steady, but not intimidating, eye contact. If you struggle with this, the way to start out is to just look at someone for a few seconds and have that smile in your eyes. What it means is to be happy to be looking at them. It's going to be conveyed through your eye contact and then move to the next person. If you're uncomfortable looking at one person for a long period, that's OK. Shift your gaze throughout the group. If it's a one-on-one conversation, you don't have to stare intently where it's uncomfortable. Smile. Look up sometimes when you're talking. Look to the side. Look at the person. If you have to shift your eye contact and then come back, that's OK. Try to make that eye contact. It's going to appear more confident and you're going to build a better connection.

Use open and assertive gestures. I'm Italian. I speak with my hands. I move a lot. I have trouble sitting during a presentation. We don't want to uncomfortably fidget. What that means is playing with our fingers. It's OK to make gestures. These are confident gestures, open gestures, authoritative gestures, and thoughtful gestures. Those are OK. What you don't want to do is start twirling your hair, picking at your nails, picking at a cuticle. I've seen it all. I've seen pulling at the threads on your clothing, playing with a button and looking down. Take up your space. Taking up all your space appears confident.

Don't be hunched. I know when you're feeling unconfident, it may be just natural to crunch up and take up as little space as possible and hide in here. You don't want to do that. Force yourself to open your posture, open up your body. When you're speaking with someone, that open posture is going to be more inviting. It's going to come across as collected, controlled, and confident. Avoid the fidgeting if you can, avoid the closed body language when you cross your arms and you're at a networking event. I look at that and I see this one's a challenge. It's like closing yourself off to the world. Don't approach me. I'm not in the mood. But when I'm standing open and I have my feet pointed toward everybody, that's like an open invitation. Come on over. When I put my feet away and I cross my arms, I look closed off. I look uncomfortable and unconfident. Remember not to cross your arms if you can help it. Don't hide your hands between your legs. Open your body language.

Another one. Facial expressions are important. A super easy one. Smile. Even a fake smile. It is proven that you can put on a fake smile, and it improves your internal confidence and it's more inviting to others. I'm not encouraging fake. You should think about it this way. When I go into an event, a speaking engagement, I think about what an opportunity. Look at this opportunity to meet all these people. Who can I help here? Who can I connect with? Start telling yourself that before you go in, and you will be in an uplifted mood. It's going to be easier to smile naturally and think of how my smile is like my business card. This is me. Nobody else has my smile. A smile is also contagious. When I see somebody smiling at me, even when I'm in a bad mood, if I'm having a bad day, I didn't get my coffee. Whatever happened, it's hard to not automatically smile back. It's proven that a smile changes the chemicals that are running through your brain. It can increase those good feeling chemicals in your brain. Smile, it's good for you, it's good for the person receiving the smile, it's inviting, and it's confident. Now, I am a little bouncy, I'm a little energetic, and that's okay. However, you can also practice some relaxed facial expressions. I do that when I'm in a business meeting. I still smile a lot, but I also relax. Take a breath before you start. That relaxed look and feeling makes you appear more confident, composed, and assured. Sitting up straight, standing up tall, and just that relaxed and open body language, that posture. Dress for success. My father always told me, you dress one step above whatever it is you're looking to achieve. If you're going in for a job where business casual is what's standard, you're going to go one step above. You don't want too far above; you don't want too far below. The other big thing, though, to remember here when you're choosing your clothes, it needs to be appropriate for whatever the event is, or the environment is. However, you always want to wear clothes that make you feel comfortable and confident. It can boost your self-esteem. If you purchase something that's extremely itchy and uncomfortable, or you're feeling like, this is not me. You will not feel as confident. I don't care what it is, even if there's a specific dress code. Put on an accessory, a cufflink, a necklace. For me, it can be a pair of shoes. It can be whatever makes you feel confident. For me, I'm a sparkly person. I like sparkle. I can dress professionally. I still have my suit; I have my heels on. I like something that makes me feel me.

I'm sparkly, shiny, and energetic. I'm Christy. You're not feeling confident right now. Here's what you remind yourself of before going in. I am, ______ (fill in the blank with your name). Here I am Christy. No one else is you. Guess what? I am so good at being Christy that I can't mess that up. Tell yourself that. It's true. You are whoever you are, and you can't mess that up. Make a mistake in a presentation. Make a mistake when interacting with a potential client, but you can't mess up being you. The other big thing to remember is to leave the requirement for somebody else's validation at the door. You are who you are. You can't mess that up. I don't need someone's validation or someone else's words to make me feel confident. I'm coming in and here's what I'm here to do. The other big thing I would recommend, you tell yourself before you go in, I'm here to focus on others. A lot of times when you're getting nervous and you're not feeling confident, it's because there's a fear of making a mistake, of what everybody's going to think of me. Even if you say, oh, I don't care what people think. Deep down, it's natural to have a fear of not meeting the expectation, not being what somebody wants you to be. People won't like me or what I have to say. It's fear. One thing I always tell people aside from reminding yourself of who you are and the fact that you can't mess that up. No matter what happens, you are still you. Can't mess that up. The other thing to remember is, it's not about you. The audience out there, let's be honest. They care about the message, the value, and what it is I'm delivering to them. Not about me. It's not about me. It's never about me. It's about what I'm going to offer them. When I go out there, I think about the audience. I think about going out there because I want to give them exactly what they need.

I came in and did a state training on office supplies. If you focus on the audience and you focus on, what can I give them that makes this valuable, that makes it worth it for them? What can I do for them? There'll be a shift in your mindset. It will now be a shift to others. When you shift your mindset from thinking about yourself and what this does for you or how I feel about it and how everybody else is going to feel about it, how's my audience going to feel? What am I going to give them? How can I help them? You will start feeling less nervous and more motivated, inspired, excited about what you're going to do. Remember, don't think about it. What if they don't like it? What if it didn't work for them? What if it works for them? Wonder if just one person in that audience walks away with something that inspires them to do something else. I didn't even give them a piece of knowledge they didn't know. But the way I said it inspired them to go act on something. That's fantastic. It's not about me. It's about everyone else. I make others my focus. Then I'm not thinking about my fears. I'm not thinking about, I wonder if I messed up. No, it's about everybody else and what I am giving to them.

Taking initiative is outside of just speaking, events, or presentations. This is just confident behaviors. At work, in the workplace, in business, with your clients. Proactively addressing tasks and problems without hesitation shows leadership and confidence. For example, volunteering for a new project or leading a discussion or speaking up when it's relevant. Not just speaking to speak, but actively listening, hearing, and then speaking to respond to that effectively. That shows taking initiative and confidence. There is a difference between aggressive and assertive communication. You don't want to be aggressive. Be assertive. Express your thoughts, feelings, and needs directly, but respectfully. That shows self-assurance and confidence. Clearly stating your opinion in a meeting or negotiating assertively, but not aggressively. Being direct, but also conveying those feelings or those thoughts professionally. Maintaining your composure. Staying calm and collected in a challenging situation. That indicates confidence in your ability to handle stress.

I had been chosen to speak. I went to a school that was K through eighth grade. They always chose the fifth or eighth grade to do the presentations for the event they did. They opened it up to everybody. I auditioned. I was in kindergarten. I was five. I was chosen. It was me, with sixth, seventh, and eighth graders. I was so excited. I was speaking about Mexico, the culture, and diversity. I went up there and it was my first big speaking event. It was when I knew this was what I wanted to do. I'm up there and I'm presenting away. I had this giant poster board up on the wall behind me. It's bigger than me. Somebody taped it or pinned it. I am only a few seconds in and the entire poster board crashes down, making a big noise echoing throughout the auditorium. My prop is down. There are all these gasps. I leaned down, picked it up, put it on the wall, and held my hand there and used the other one to point the entire time while I finished that presentation.

Managing unexpected issues during a presentation without panic shows confidence. If you mess up *and you will mess up*, nobody remembers it or cares. You're in a presentation. Only you care. Make it about everybody else. If you get caught up, a trick is to either A, make quick light of it. Humor is always a way to shrug things off. I can speak this morning. I need more coffee and then move on quickly. To your point or just don't address it. Take a breath and start over. Nobody's going to remember that hiccup. Handling unexpected issues, even in work, a conflict, maintaining composure and calm is important. That's back to that self-regulation. Positive body language. Practice it and it will become natural. Maintaining good eye contact. Even if you must look up, away, down, it doesn't matter. Coming back and making sure they know that you're interested.

Deciding decisively. Even in an uncertain situation, it reflects confidence in your judgment when you're able to decide quickly. Choosing a course of action without excessive hesitation. It doesn't mean you don't analyze, but it means sometimes you need to make a quick decision and by doing it and using these other techniques, you appear confident. Another confident behavior is admitting mistakes and learning from them. Owning up to errors. Using them as learning opportunities, not only for yourself, but for others. It shows confidence in your ability to grow. If I make a mistake when I'm presenting, like I said, sometimes I'll highlight it. If I make a mistake in a project, I come forward and say, well, look at what I did. Let's propose a solution. Being able to admit that we all make mistakes, that you are not perfect, that I am human like everybody else, that displays confidence. Another confident behavior is welcoming challenges. Don't shy away from them. Embracing new challenges is an exciting opportunity to grow and learn and demonstrate self-assurance. Taking on a new challenging client. Even when I don't always know exactly what I'm doing. I welcome new challenges. I don't hide from them.

Another one is setting and respecting boundaries. Knowing your own limits and asserting them respectfully shows self-respect and confidence. Saying no to something professionally. There's a way to say it. I have a whole series on professional speech and how to convey exactly what you're thinking professionally. But that is something that is important and it's a confidence building skill. Engaging actively with others. Take part in conversations. Show genuine interest in others' ideas. That shows confidence in a social setting. It doesn't have to be all about you. I want to hear from my audience when I'm speaking. I love interactive opportunities because I want to hear what their concerns are. I'm going to pivot and change a bit of what I'm going to speak, based on what the audience is telling me. How are they responding? Listening to others and their ideas helps expand my knowledge.

My perspective helps me open up more. It's important in confidence building. Another confidence building behavior to practice is giving and receiving feedback gracefully. Being open to constructive criticism and offering thoughtful feedback professionally shows confidence in your ability to improve. Discussing performance reviews constructively, having those tough conversations with team members, having them with clients, practicing them in your everyday life, just giving feedback and receiving feedback. When someone says something to me, or I solicit feedback. I really want to hear it. When I say to my team, I want you to tell me what you thought of that. Those who have been around for a while know that I'm being sincere. I want you to tell me exactly where you would improve. If I did something successful, great. High five me. If there was an opportunity to do it even better, I would want to know that. Learn to take every piece of feedback you get. Analyze it and determine if there is truth to it. If there is, use that to improve, to get better.

Next, we're going to talk a bit about enhancing empathy. The first piece of enhancing empathy is active listening, focusing fully on someone who's speaking, avoiding distractions, showing that you're listening through nods and verbal affirmations. Show them and not just where you're zoned out and nodding blindly. Listen to what they're saying, put the phone down, and focus on others, focus on what they're saying with an intent not to respond, but to hear what it is they're conveying. Understand it. Restate or rephrase things you've heard throughout to ensure you understand. Engage in that conversation.

How to Become More Likeable

Let's jump into how to become more likable. You might say, "You just talked about being authentic. Why would we want to change our behavior to be more likable?" It's not that you don't want to be yourself, but when you are communicating with someone in business, when you are looking to have that energy that you bring to a room, to a party, to an event, whether it's networking, speaking, or presenting in a room of coworkers, it doesn't matter. To make people more receptive to what you're about to share, you want to be likable. We all want that. We're going to look at the whiteboard and walk through some of the most common things you can do to become more likable. The first one is to show genuine interest in others. People appreciate it when they feel heard, when they feel valued. Show genuine interest in what others have to say. Listening, not just to respond or to form a response, but listening to understand what people are conveying. Show genuine interest in what others say, make them feel valued, heard, and validated. Number two, this is one I had to learn. We want to listen more than we speak. Being a good listener is crucial. It shows that you value others' perspectives, opinions, and contribution to the conversation. When you're listening, to understand, to empathize, you want to listen more than you speak. Don't listen with an intent to respond immediately or how can I add to this? If you truly have something to add, that's fine, but you want to make it a rule to listen more than you speak.

Give your full attention, summarize what you've heard, and here's where you can add insights or really ask questions. That's a big one. I like to ask questions, engage further, and really show that I was listening. I was invested in the conversation. Questions help me clarify what I was understanding, what I heard. Another thing is to be positive and upbeat. I have many people that come to me and ask, "Christy, how can I become a better speaker? How can I become more magnetic and charismatic? How can I make people like me more?" Just having a positive and upbeat attitude. It doesn't have to be cheerleader sounding, just positive. It's like smiles. People are drawn to other people who have a positive outlook on things, and they can really lift everybody's spirit. Why are people drawn to others with energy, to people who are positive? They're not complaining. It's one thing to connect over a complaint, but you want to do it positively. When you have that energy, that excitement, that positivity that's shining outward, it's going to act like a magnet and pull people into you. Even when things don't go right, you can practice responding positively to those incidents.

Another thing, number four, is going to be using people's names more. Now, you don't want to overuse it to where it sounds ridiculous or not authentic, but using someone's name in conversation it makes the interaction more personal. It shows that you value them. You remembered their names. You're connecting with them individually.

You're addressing that specific person. They're important. Names make people feel you're listening, like they're important because they are. Attempt to remember names if you can, especially at networking events, at places where you're going to meet new people. Use them in conversation. What's an interest of his? What's something he does in his work? You know, when you're listening to people or you're meeting people, note something unique about them or something that they have an interest in. When you're listening to listen, you're going to hear a lot of clues about, they like this, or somebody might mention that they do this on the side, or they do this outside of work. Use that and associate that with the person's name. If you can rhyme, or put something in a song, great. Our minds memorize musical melodies and rhyming words, easier than just random facts. Connect them to something. Then you can bring that up later the next time you see them. That's going to mean a lot to that person. It's going to make them feel they were important. You remembered their name, and that little tidbit about them. That's a great thing to practice daily. I was shopping the other day. The person at the register came up to me and said, "Hi, can I help you with anything today?" I said, "Oh, just browsing." She said, "Oh, great. My name's Amber. If you need anything, just let me know." Amber, the color of her eyes, reminded me of an amber color. That's how I connected that. I remembered she had on a pretty pair of earrings that were, again, that amber color. I went out to the counter later to pay and addressed her by name. "Amber, thank you so much for asking. I love your earrings." An authentic compliment. Don't make something up, make it authentic. But I used that to make myself remember her name so that I could use it later.

Number five, mirror body language. When you mirror body language, it's a way to build rapport. This does not mean going overboard. That can look like mocking or mimicking too much where it stands out and people think there's something wrong. Mirror body language in a minor way, something little that they do, and that creates that sense of familiarity and comfort. It creates a connection between you and the other person. Makes you more likable because it's comfortable. We do it ourselves. We see somebody else doing it and I can totally be friends with this person. I can totally connect with this person. They're very similar to me and people gravitate toward similarities. Do some mirroring, and you can practice this daily with people you meet out in public or in virtual meetings, with coworkers, family members, or wherever you are.

Number six, this is big. Smile and show warmth. Don't just smile with your mouth. Smiling with your mouth and your eyes not matching can look fake. To have that authentic smile, that infectious smile that's contagious, you want to also smile with your eyes. It's a simple gesture. A smile is a universal language. It does not matter what the individual's primary language is. If you're smiling at someone, they understand. You've made a connection. It makes you more approachable. It makes you appear friendly, warm, and positive. All those things we talked about that make you more magnetic, that draw people to you. That's what you want. Smile and show that warmth. We talked a lot about showing empathy and understanding. This is on here again, under the likability list. Empathy builds a deeper connection. When you can put yourself in someone else's shoes, and really understand what it is they feel, think, like, and want, that builds a great connection. It shows that you can share in their feelings. Understand what it is they want. Even in business, in a sales situation, we're not even talking about basic networking, but in a sales situation. How important is it to put yourself in your customer's shoes and really understand what it is they're looking to achieve? What's their goal? What do they want? What keeps them up at night? Understanding that is going to help you better position your product or service to match their exact needs, to be the solution they're looking for. It's so important when you're developing marketing material, when you're developing sales and marketing strategies, understanding what your audience wants, being able to listen to people and really develop ways to speak to them that target their feelings. We talk about grabbing attention by evoking emotion. It's a big one. Piquing curiosity and then creating relatability, creating something that they can relate to. That's how you grab someone's attention. To do that, you need to understand your audience and you need to put yourself in your customer's shoes.

Be open and authentic. Many people ask me, “Christy, you're saying be authentic, be myself, but then you're telling me, this is the list to follow, how to be more likable, to change myself.” It's not to change yourself. It's to bring out another side of yourself. Let's be honest. We are not just a one-person, simple thing. We don't have one simple emotion or side of ourselves. We're more complex than that. We have many sides, and the side that we show in a specific situation is typically what's necessary at that moment. Like we talked about charisma and confidence being a choice. Who you are at that moment is a choice. It does not mean that you're not you. You are who you are at your core, your core values, what makes you unique. You will not change those things. If you're changing those things, that's a problem. You should not shift your core beliefs, morals, ethics, or mission. What changes is the way you're presenting something. You're tailoring it to the needs of the individual or group you're with. That does not make you less authentic.

There's a difference. You're not changing who you are at your core. You are changing how you present yourself in a specific situation to be appropriate. Again, we're multidimensional humans. We have many sides. Be open and authentic. Authenticity builds trust. Being true to those core values invites those around you to also be their unique and genuine self. Being unique and letting that show through encourages others to do the same. People like it. They're attracted to that. Another one is to offer genuine compliments. I want to stop right there and emphasize the word genuine. You don't want to flatter someone. We're using genuine compliments. A compliment is a great way to open a conversation, connect with someone. When you're meeting someone new, it's a great way to brighten someone's day. Don't you feel good when you receive a compliment? Of course you do. It makes you more likable. People like people that like something about them and vocalize that. But choose something that you truly like. Make it authentic. I do not flatter people. I found something about the person that I like. For example, we're going to rewind back to where I was at the store recently. I was shopping, and I met Amber. I really liked Amber's earrings. I would have worn them myself, and they look fantastic with her eyes. I complimented that because it was authentic. They're going to pick up on that. People like being complimented when it's truthful and authentic.

Avoid controversial topics. When I say avoid controversial topics, that means in a first-time interaction, you don't want to bring up something extremely controversial. You don't know that person. That could be something that builds a wall immediately rather than opens that connection to build on. If you build a wall from moment one, you've alienated that person. You will not make the connection. You will not come across as charismatic or magnetic. Controversial topics can draw a lot of attention to yourself and your brand, which can be a good thing when it's not offensive. I usually recommend if you are in a business setting, you'll want to steer away from discussions about politics, things that are just not appropriate in the workplace. That doesn't mean that you're not your authentic self. It means you choose not to discuss that topic at that moment. Instead, focus on the common ground items, shared interests in the conversation. Listen more than you're speaking. You're picking up on interests. You're picking up on little things about that person and you're going to find something you can connect on, or you want to hear more about so that there is a connection to build upon, something that you have in common.

A sense of humor. Everybody likes a good sense of humor. Make interactions more enjoyable, more memorable. Sometimes when I'm speaking on stage, I will use some humor. When I'm telling a story, especially a personal story, when I'm adding something, I'm a sarcastic individual outside of work. You're going to hear a bit of sarcasm sprinkled in when I'm speaking or training, even just when I'm interacting. But you want to be cautious here as well. It should be appropriate. Sometimes humor is not appropriate. Let's steer away from humor when we're on a serious subject. Now, sometimes it's okay to throw some in to break that up a bit or dissolve tension, but you want to be mindful of how that other person is feeling. Put yourself in their shoes. Use that empathetic listening skill to determine whether it's appropriate to insert humor. This one you want to be cautious of. Be funny, lighthearted, again, nothing offensive, and you want to be very aware of your audience and the setting. If we are discussing a very somber topic, unless you really want to break through the tension, it's not an appropriate time to insert a random joke. Use discernment here.

Be inclusive in a group setting. You're going to be more likable when you're including people, and I've found that I can be at an event. I was speaking at a summit, and I noticed the groups were very segmented. There were little clusters of three and four people, and there were several new people that came into the room. They showed up a bit later than the rest of us. They were speaking later in the summit, and they were standing awkwardly at the door. I waved them over. Everybody wants to feel included. Making them feel included, especially in a group setting, in a conversation is going to make you more likable. Practice that by drawing new people in. If you see somebody standing over there, if you're in a conversation, open the conversation. But for now, just know that inclusivity, inviting people in, making them feel wanted, part of the group, valued, just included, is going to make you more likable, and it's just good practice. The more people we bring in, the better it is. Introduce yourself to more people more often.

Being likable, it's not about flattery. It's not just about impressing people, and it's not about being the center of attention. When we talk about being magnetic, pulling people into you, that does not mean that you must be the center of attention, the spotlight only, nobody else can have a chance. It's very much the opposite. It's all about others. The way to make yourself more magnetic, likable, and charismatic is to focus on others. It's about making others feel included, comfortable, and valued. When you're there and you make others feel good, then you're going to be likable and everyone's going to gravitate toward you. Be the person who walks in and lights up the room, or the one that you see at a networking event, and everybody wants to go up and meet them. Or a speaker. Everybody's rushing to the side of the stage to talk to them afterward. Remember, charisma, confidence, and likability are choices, it's a set of behaviors. Just having that spark. It's based on your behaviors, and on your output toward others. If you take nothing else away from this, I want you to take away that to make yourself more likable; you put your focus on everyone around you, not yourself. Making others feel good, valued, included, comfortable, uplifting them, empowering them. That's how you become truly likable. If you take nothing else away, focus on others, focus on how you make others feel.

Techniques to Build Instant Rapport

We are going to cover reading people. Time to dive into the human psyche. We are going to talk about reading people and some things to look for when you are reading different people in different situations. In the world of business, it's so important and such an advantage if you can understand the person across from you. Whether that's in sales, marketing, advertising, at a networking event, speaking with team members, or customers, it doesn't matter. If you can understand the person across from you, then it's going to make all the difference. It's just going to help you become that much more successful in your business.

You know, decoding what somebody is thinking or feeling beyond what they're saying to you is really going to help you get better at every aspect of the business. That's what we're diving into today. Why is it important? Think about it in a negotiation. If you're able to read your counterparts, it can help steer the conversation to your advantage. When you're selling, understanding your clients' unspoken cues and how they're saying things, not just what they're saying to you can really transform how you manage that sales process, how you custom tailor the solution, pivot, and adjust your pitch. A leader listening to a team member allows you to really hone in on those cues, the unspoken ones, especially, and transform the way you manage or lead your team.

The way you lead your team, your contractors, or your business initiatives can help you become someone they trust. It can help you tailor your approach to match exactly what they need. This is something you can practice in your everyday life. It's picking up on subtle signs and signals, hesitation in a voice, excitement in someone's eyes or their expression, nervous tapping of a foot, things like that. We're going to start with some of the verbal cues. These are easier to notice. The first one is the tone of the voice. Changes in a tone of voice when someone's talking can show someone's true feelings or intentions. Regardless of what words I'm using or what I'm saying, the way I say it impacts how you respond or how you take that phrase. It can really tell us what this person's emotional state is, what their confidence level is, and what their intention is. We want to pay attention not just to what they're saying, but how they're saying it. Is their tone consistent with the words they're using? Does it change when certain topics are mentioned? If you're talking with a potential client and they're excited, and suddenly their tone goes a little stiffer, more bored, or their tone falls, or there's that hesitation. They were talking quickly, and they're excited, and they're forging forward, and then their breath is catching. They're hesitating. They're thinking. They're pausing a lot. Suddenly, they might be filled with doubt about whatever you just said. Let me drill down into that. Let me either adjust the way I'm pitching to this person, or let me clarify what I just said, or let me ask some questions to drill down and get to the concern so we can get it now before it becomes a no later in the sales pitch. Some tones of voice that you might encounter in a conversation, hesitant or uncertain. That can suggest doubt, lack of confidence, and sometimes it's just unfamiliarity with the topic. Sometimes it can indicate to us we've gone too far, too fast in an explanation with someone, and they're now unfamiliar with the topic we're talking about or less familiar with what you're discussing, and we might need to rewind a little or explain a little more thoroughly. This can be useful in any conversation, but especially negotiations, decision-making situations help you identify different points of concern. Another tone, assertive, and obviously indicates self-assurance in leadership or sales. This can signal a powerful belief in whatever message you're conveying.

Another tone to watch for is agitated or frustrated. If it's in a customer, are they becoming frustrated with the situation? Are they becoming agitated? Is it one of your team members and they're becoming frustrated with something going on at work with a project? Are they becoming agitated with what you're conveying to them? Do you need to adjust how you're delivering the message? You know, agitation or frustration can indicate a lot of things, from annoyance, dissatisfaction, to impatience. It's very important in customer service, in speaking with your clients, or with your team members for conflict resolution. We want to identify what that source of frustration is. Another tone to keep an eye out for is enthusiastic. Obviously, we know what that means, especially in a sales presentation or within your team. They're excited about a project. It can really show what resonates most with your audience. When you're speaking, when you're training, is someone getting excited when you're presenting something at work on a project? Well, that seems to resonate most with them. It got their attention. They're excited about what you're saying. A soothing tone is another one. They're relaxed. They're confident. They feel in control of the situation. Another tone might be monotone or flat. Are they bored? Are they disengaged? Is this a networking event, and they've zoned out because you've lost them in the conversation, and you really need to say something that sparks their attention again? Is it during a sales presentation, and somebody's literally fallen asleep on the inside? We need to wake them back up, pull them back in, get them excited about what it is we're providing. We want to really watch for that monotone or flat tone. A warmer, friendly tone shows openness, approachability at a networking event, within a sales pitch, and within the team. They're open and willing to listen to what you're about to deliver message-wise.

Skeptical tones. This is going to have more of that high-pitched question at the end. Might be some disbelief where they trail off in what they're saying. They might be more hesitant about what they're saying. Skepticism can be conveyed in tone. It's a little more uncertain, a little slower. Things like that you want to watch for. Fast-paced or rapid. Is the person excited? Are they nervous? Is there a time constraint? Do they need something right away and they're speaking quickly about it? That might mean that this is something on their radar as an urgent matter that you can address in that manner. Another one is slower, more deliberate. Depending on what they're saying, you must look at it as a holistic approach, but it could suggest thoughtfulness, caution, hesitancy, skepticism, or just emphasis.

Sometimes when we're speaking, it could just mean a specific emphasis on certain words to emphasize the importance or to grab their attention. It's like an attention grabber in the brain. Another one is soft-spoken or gentle. They're shy, not confident in this conversation. They're uncomfortable, quiet people. It's non-confrontational. They're just listening, hearing you out. Another tone to watch for is loud or forceful. That can indicate enthusiasm, anger, or a desire to dominate the conversation, and that is significant when you're speaking with a team member or a potential client. If they feel the need to dominate that conversation, that may be something that you want to be cognizant of so that you can let them feel they are leading and have control of that conversation while you're leading them along the trail. It is important to recognize that. This is so important in every aspect of what you do in business, whether it's networking, speaking, training, you're interacting with a mentor, a team member, or a client. Really focus on the way they're saying something as well as what they're saying to ensure that you tailor your response, your sales pitch, your attempt to connect at an event with what's going to elicit positive vocal responses. If you're not sure, but you're listening, you're picking up on these subtle tones and pitches, ask some open-ended questions to learn a bit more about that, or you might understand right away that their tone has shifted.

Really think about that, analyze it, and understand why. Should you ask open-ended questions? Change the topic? Dig deeper? Are they excited, and should you continue on this path? Adjusting to their cues helps guide your next move. Another key factor is speaking patterns—the speed, rhythm, volume, and tone of speech. These can reflect if someone is confident, anxious, or bored. For instance, frequent pauses or *ums* might suggest uncertainty, while a flat tone could indicate they're disengaged. Pay attention to pitch variation. A varied pitch keeps conversations engaging, while a monotone suggests detachment, requiring you to adjust your approach. Frequent interruptions may show impatience or eagerness—this is a chance to ask an open-ended question to clarify their thoughts. Smooth turn-taking usually indicates strong conversational skills and confidence.

We talked a bit about that question inflection, that upward inflection, if they're ending on a high note, on a sound that sounds like they're asking something like that, it can be a sign of uncertainty, of them seeking approval, so we want to be listening for that, or we hear a downward inflection. That can indicate they're certain about this. They're assertive in what they're saying right now, they have a very strong opinion formed around this subject. That's important, and then again, listening for their emphasis placed on certain words, so they're emphasizing specific words, they're slowing it down right there, emphasizing certain words can change the meaning of a sentence, and so just because we're hearing them say a set of words, we want to also listen to what words they're focused on, what's important to them when they're conveying a thought, or when they're responding to a question that you've asked. Watch for body language—open posture, relaxed arms, and uncrossed legs suggest someone is receptive to your message. But if they cross their arms or legs, it could signal defensiveness or discomfort. In a sales discussion, this might mean it's time to adjust your approach.

Leaning in or out is another key cue. If someone leans in, they're engaged. If they lean back, it may mean they're losing interest or distancing themselves from the conversation—especially in sales. Adjust your approach if you notice them inching away. Hand gestures can also reveal a lot. Open palms and upward gestures often suggest honesty and engagement, while pointed or chopping motions might seem aggressive or just emphasize a point. Watch how they move their hands and body to gauge their receptiveness.

Facial touching, like touching the mouth or nose, can sometimes indicate doubt or discomfort. But remember, it could just be a habit—context is key. Some people fidget by playing with their hair or picking at a lip, so watch for shifts in behavior. Smiling is another important cue. A genuine smile involves the eyes, not just the mouth. If someone's smile is real, you'll see it in their eyes, which shows warmth and engagement. Another one is eye contact, you want to look at it individually, as we talked about, you want to have some varied eye motion, but consistent eye contact can indicate confidence in the individual, and honesty, a lack of eye contact, gauge the situation, but it can sometimes suggest discomfort. If you see a shift in their behavior, so they were making consistent eye contact, but suddenly they're looking away, they're looking down, they don't want to make that eye contact, they might be uncomfortable, they might be evading, they don't really want to talk about this. It can also be a lack of confidence in this area of conversation. Too much eye contact can be aggressive or confrontational. You don't want to stare somebody down, and if they're doing that, that can be a sign of them attempting to assert control in this situation. It can be an aggressive behavior coming out.

Micro-expressions—those quick, involuntary facial movements—can reveal a lot, but you have to be observant to catch them. For example, a quick furrow of the brow might show confusion or disagreement. Always interpret body language in context. Look at what they're saying, how they're saying it, and what their body is doing. Everyone's unique, so watch for shifts in behavior—whether in tone, volume, or demeanor. These changes will help you assess whether your message is landing effectively. Don't make a judgment based on one gesture, one expression, look for a pattern and look for the shifts or changes as you talk. The key is practice. Start observing people in everyday situations—whether you're with family, at work, on a Zoom call, or even at the grocery store. The more you expose yourself to different people and settings, the better you'll get at picking up on those subtle behavior shifts.

Develop self-awareness by paying attention to your own body language and how you speak. When you're on the phone, try putting a mirror in front of you and watch how your facial expressions change as you talk. This helps you notice your own cues, which makes it easier to recognize them in others during real-life conversations. Using this holistic approach—focusing on both what's being said and non-verbal cues—will help you better tailor your interactions. Practice this week by paying attention to eye contact—whether you're talking to someone or checking yourself in a mirror. Notice if the person is giving direct eye contact or avoiding it. Is it friendly or assertive? Also, try mirroring the other person's eye contact style (without overdoing it) to build rapport. People naturally connect with those who seem familiar. Mirroring subtle expressions or body language can strengthen your connection with others.

Many people focus so much on what they're going to say that they forget to listen to understand. This means they miss out on subtle cues, which can hurt communication. In business, understanding these cues can drastically improve your negotiations, relationship-building, and sales. Practice listening with full attention—it'll give you an edge over your competition. You'll notice that the same skills for reading people also help when building rapport—body language, posture, eye contact—all come into play. When meeting someone, the goal is to build a connection. Use mirroring techniques, mimicking body language or speech patterns subtly. Observe their mood—if it's a serious topic, adjust accordingly. Don't be overly upbeat if they're sharing something sensitive. It's not about being negative, but about matching the tone to make them feel understood and connected.

Another way to build instant rapport is to employ active listening. Listen, concentrate, understand, and respond to what's being said. Don't listen to just respond. Don't be forming your response as they're speaking. Listen first, then respond. Nod in agreement if it's appropriate. Use affirmative words to encourage the person to continue with their discussion. Ask open-ended questions to show them you're listening and engaged. You're interested in this topic. Open with a warm, genuine smile. When it's appropriate during the conversation, you want to have that smile. Smiling triggers a good feeling within ourselves when we smile. It also triggers the right brain chemicals to make the other person feel uplifted and happier. Another great way to build rapport is to share relatable stories. Personal experiences help create a bond. For example, I shared my struggle with eye contact—opening up about something personal makes interactions memorable. Listen carefully, and if you pick up on something relatable, share a brief story to strengthen that connection.

Show empathy by expressing that you understand and share their feelings. Simple phrases like "I can imagine how that felt" or "That must have been really challenging" help you connect on a deeper level. Let them know you understand their emotions, building a strong connection. Find common ground by identifying shared interests or experiences. Listen carefully to the conversation for clues and build on any commonalities. People naturally connect when they find something in common, whether it's a shared experience or interest. Use positive body language to convey openness and interest. Avoid crossing your arms, and nod to show you're engaged in the conversation (without overdoing it!). Maintain eye contact, but keep it friendly with a warm smile.

Emotional Intelligence Unlock Social Smarts Your Sixth Sense

Let's start with the basics of emotional intelligence, or as we're going to refer to it here on out, are social smarts, your sixth sense. What is emotional intelligence? We hear it a lot. It's this new buzzword that's thrown around in business. I hear a lot of discussions about it. It's all over social media. Everybody says, EI or EQ, Emotional Intelligence. What is it? It's the ability to understand and manage your own emotions and those of the surrounding people. When we break it down, that's what emotional intelligence is. Think of EQ or social smarts as a toolkit, and it has five key tools in that toolkit. Self-awareness, self-regulation, motivation, empathy, and your social skills. Let's break them down. Self-awareness is like your internal mirror. It's knowing your emotions, strengths, and weaknesses—and how they affect your actions. This is crucial because without self-awareness, it's hard to understand others' emotions. Take time to reflect: what are you great at? Where do you struggle? Write it down and think about how it impacts your decisions and behavior.

Self-regulation is all about managing your emotions once you've identified your strengths, weaknesses, and triggers. It's about staying calm and in control, even when things around you aren't. You can't control other people or situations, but you can control how you respond. Focus on managing your own reactions—that's what will influence those around you. A gigantic piece of that is self-awareness, your identification piece, and then self-regulation. You need to understand and accept that you can't control other people, things around you, but you can control how you respond, react, and what you do in those situations. How you control that, how you drive that can influence and inspire the surrounding individuals to behave a specific way.

Motivation is your inner drive—what keeps you pushing toward your goals, even when challenges and roadblocks appear. It's the force that keeps you moving forward.

The fourth key in your toolkit is empathy. Empathy is like stepping into someone else's shoes. There is a big difference between empathy and sympathy. Empathy is understanding someone else's emotions, their motivations, what drives them, and using that understanding in your actions with those individuals to guide where you want to go. Empathy is really stepping inside someone else's shoes and understanding the why behind what drives them, what they're doing, and their decision-making. This is significant later, in sales and marketing.

Social skills are the ability to build networks, navigate social situations, and lead with influence. Often called *people skills*, these are essential for business owners to practice and refine daily. Strong social skills enable you to inspire others and accomplish tasks, even in areas where you lack expertise.

Think of social smarts as the hidden melody in a song—the thing that makes it stand out. In business, social smarts make leaders shine. Charisma isn't luck; it's your social smarts at work. Many new business owners focus on sales, marketing, and finances, but without sharp social skills and emotional intelligence, success in those areas becomes harder to reach. When you're self-aware—knowing your strengths, weaknesses, emotions, and triggers—you naturally come across as authentic. People are drawn to genuine leaders. I've had people suggest I tone down my energy to be taken more seriously, but when I stray from what makes me confident, I'm less successful. Being self-aware doesn't mean you can't adjust. It's not about being inauthentic; it's about being your best business self and honing your skills. With practice, you'll exude authenticity naturally as you understand what drives you. Self-regulation helps you stay composed during crises and negotiations, earning respect from your team and customers. Losing your cool leads to rash decisions and damages your credibility as a leader or business owner. Motivated leaders inspire their teams, creating an environment where everyone's striving for excellence. You're able to inspire your team and motivate them to perform.

Now, let's talk about sales and marketing. Without strong sales and marketing, growing your business to seven or eight figures is tough. The key is tuning into your customers' needs, pain points, and desires, then crafting messages that resonate on a deeper level. People buy from people, not just brands. Yes, they buy brands, but ultimately, it's the connection they feel with the people behind the brand that seals the deal. Social smarts help build a brand that people trust and connect with, strengthening brand authority and awareness. In today's digital age, brand authority is crucial. Your brand needs to connect, inspire, and resonate with people. In networking, your social smarts act as a magnet, drawing people in, opening doors, and expanding opportunities. If you want your business to grow, connect with more people more often—both online and in person. Don't focus on making a sale right away, simply connect. The more connections you make, the more your network and opportunities grow.

As you expand your network, you gain access to more resources, knowledge, and opportunities. Most successful brands didn't rely on luck; they relied on networking. It's all about who you know and how you connect. People naturally gravitate toward those who inspire and motivate them. That doesn't mean avoiding challenges—it's about addressing them in a positive, uplifting way. No one wants to stick around someone who's always negative. Be the one who brings energy and optimism to every interaction. Go to these events and be motivated, inspired, connect with people, get excited. That's really what you want to portray. Then, with leadership, as you scale, you are going to need to lean on team members or build teams, or even if it's outsourced, build networks of resources. Connect with other leaders. Have mentors. Have leadership partners, buddies. It's important to consider other perspectives when we're scaling in business. Social Smarts is the cornerstone here. It's about leading with empathy, motivating the team, driving your business towards success with that human touch. Your social smarts—your sixth sense—are powerful whether you're closing a sale, building a brand, networking, or leading a team. They give you that edge and make you, and your brand, stand out. We'll break down the skills and practice tips to help open doors and grow your business. But it's not just about business growth—it's about expanding your social smarts to the next level, so you can work wonders in your business.

Crafting Messages that Stick and Resonate

We're going to go over crafting messages that stick and resonate. Designing a message that sticks doesn't require a big speech or presentation. It could be a simple conversation, meeting someone new, or networking. The goal is to make yourself memorable—and that starts with understanding people. The first thing to remember when creating a memorable message is to know your audience. Even if you're meeting someone for the first time, pay attention to their behavior. In just a few minutes, you can learn a lot. When preparing a business message or speaking at an event, know your audience. Tailor your message to their interests and needs. Speak to them as if you're talking to one person, not a crowd. It doesn't matter if you're speaking to 10,000 people—speak as if you're talking to just one person. When I spoke at a state training with 5,000 people, I focused on one ideal audience member. Each person is there to hear something valuable, and your message should resonate with each of them. When you're speaking, don't speak broadly. Don't speak to the masses. Speak like you're speaking to one person, your one ideal audience member. If you can, if you're going to speak at an event, this would not apply to when you're meeting a stranger, conduct audience research, create personas to better align your message. Look at what your audience preference is. What is their preferred method of delivery? This goes for sales, the same way it does creating your message. Just like when you're crafting a sales offer, you're sitting there thinking of who's your ideal client is. What is psychographics? What are the demographics behind that? Who makes up the specific person for whom you have a solution? The same thing when you're speaking, you want to tailor your approach to exactly to whom you're going to be delivering the message. Know your audience.

Storytelling is powerful and memorable. It doesn't have to be long—just something relatable. For example, I often start presentations with simple, shared experiences, like the hassle of airport travel or needing a coffee by 11 a.m. These relatable stories connect with your audience. Use real-life examples and firsthand experiences to illustrate your key points. Throughout this book, I share my own successes, mistakes, and personal stories. The key is to make sure your story aligns with your message. Don't just share for the sake of sharing—make it meaningful.

When creating a message that resonates, simplicity is key. Keep it clear and concise. Avoid complex language. You may know a topic well, but can you explain it so that someone who isn't an expert can still take value from it? The goal is to make your message accessible to everyone, even if they don't share your level of experience. I always tell my kids, "Keep it simple, stupid," to make sure the message is easy to understand.

Emotional appeal makes messages stick. Use language that stirs feelings like excitement, motivation, or empathy. Even in a group, connect with individuals by explaining the feelings behind your message. To grab attention, remember the three keys: pique curiosity, evoke emotion, and make it relatable. People remember emotions. Think back to childhood—many memories are tied to how you felt in those moments. My first speaking engagement was at age five. My poster board fell, and everyone thought I'd cry. But I picked it up and kept going. That rush of excitement and achievement is still with me, and that's how I knew I wanted to empower others. Emotions make experiences memorable, so use them to create connections.

Repetition helps people remember key points. Studies show we only retain a fraction of what we hear, but repetition can boost retention. Throughout this book, you'll notice themes repeated to make them stick. Use repetition, catchy phrases, or slogans to emphasize your main ideas. That's why skilled speakers often repeat key phrases—they make the message more memorable. Another thing you can do, if it's appropriate, is to incorporate visuals. Visual aids can enhance your brain's ability to recall the message or material. Use images, graphs, or charts. Sometimes I've gone up and used just a prop. It can be something small. It can be a coffee mug that has a specific message on it. I've taken tap shoes up on stage and used that as an analogy, but it's memorable. When I'm speaking, I'm usually not sitting, but moving around and the gestures and something you did in that moment can draw attention back in. It can re-grab that attention, hook it back in. It can also stick better in that person's mind when they walk away. Me getting up with my tap shoes first; it drew attention. Second, when I'm showing the tap shoe or I'm talking about the story or I'm putting it on and showing specific muscle memory, it's memorable. They remember, oh yeah, that's the woman that was up there with the tap shoes. That's that old person who still gets up and dances. It's memorable.

Interactive elements make your message stick. Engage your audience by asking open-ended questions or using a call to action. When you involve them, it's more memorable. I've called out to volunteers or asked relatable questions to keep people engaged. Another key is consistency—make sure your message is unified across presentations, emails, social media, or advertisements. Keeping things consistent helps reinforce your message.

Use the rule of three to organize your message. People remember information in sets of three—beginning, middle, and end. Make sure each part conveys something important. Start strong to grab attention, end memorably, and keep the middle focused. Also, practice. Deliver your message, seek feedback, and keep refining. Honest feedback is key to improvement. I always ask my team for their actual opinions, not just flattery, because that's how we all grow.

Actionable tips and insights bring value. The most memorable messages connect with your audience on a personal and emotional level. Even with mundane topics, like discussing office supplies at a training, I made the message engaging by relating it to their everyday experiences. People may not remember every detail, but they'll remember how it made them feel. That's the power of making things relatable.

Let's talk about charisma and its role in persuasion and influence. Charisma isn't about being the most outgoing person—it's about how you make others feel. It's relational. The person who lights up a room does so by making others feel energized and valued. Charisma comes from confidence, authenticity, positivity, and warmth. Focus on genuine connections by showing interest in others—their ideas, feelings, and needs. When you do that, people naturally feel drawn to you.

The second point to remember is that confidence is key to charisma. What is confidence? A choice. A set of behaviors. Confidence isn't a personality trait. You hear me reiterate this because I want you to remember that and take that away. I want you to know that it's not something you're born with. It's a skill. It's a set of behaviors you show. Confidence is key to charisma. You will not have this person who has that spark, has that energy, lights up the room, and they're unconfident. No, no, they're going to appear confident. They're going to display confident behaviors. But it must be balanced with humility. To be that person who draws people to them, that inspires and motivates, that everyone wants to be around, you need to have confidence without arrogance. There's a difference. Confidence is a demonstrated set of behaviors. It's how you handle yourself. It's understanding your ability and conveying the fact that you're confident in that ability to others, but it's not arrogant. You will never think if you're a confident person, a true, confident person will not feel they are above people or better at things than others. They have a distinct perspective. They're confident in knowing that this is my ability. I'm confident about that. I don't need it validated. This is what it is, but it's not arrogant. You never think you're above or better than anyone. Practice self-assured body language and speech while remaining approachable and humble. Give off that feeling of comfortable confidence, but you want to be open and approachable. You want people to feel welcome to come up to you. You don't want to just be the person who people are like; I want to be around them. Make those people feel like, come on over. You're welcome here.

Some tips for developing that charisma. We talked about listening because people are drawn to individuals that listen, actively listen. They're respectful in their understanding. They are developing your charisma. It's important to work on your emotional intelligence, your EQ. I call it social smarts, your sixth sense. Being attuned to your own emotions and others' emotions around you. That enhances your charisma. Practice recognizing and responding to both your own emotions and to the emotions of those around you. Positive body language, your warm smile, your appropriate eye contact, your open posture, which can significantly boost your charismatic presence. How you present yourself, your body language, your posture. Remember, we want to work on that. Engaging storytelling, stories that captivate, connect with people. You don't want to just spit out facts. You don't want to be robotic. How many times have you gone somewhere, and you meet someone or you're listening to someone speak and they're so intelligent and there is so much value in what they're saying, but it's hard to pay attention and you walk away with, what was that again? Be memorable. Use relevant personal stories. Personal things to connect with and bond with the audience. Use that to illustrate the key points. Use that to be memorable and convey a message. Express genuine enthusiasm. You do not have to be a cheerleader. You do not have to be as bouncy as I am. Be yourself, but have that genuine enthusiasm for what it is you're there to do or what you're there to convey. Just like your smile. Enthusiasm is contagious. When you're passionate about something, it shows, and it can inspire others. How do you think teams are inspired? It's that passion that comes from the top. It must come from a genuine leader within the team. That's not a position, that's not a title, a leader. It's the way you behave, the way you lead, your actions that make you a leader, not your title. A genuine leader can show their passion, their enthusiasm for something. It's so contagious that inspires others to want to follow along, to jump on board, to be so excited. I'm passionate about what I do. I get so excited about it. People say, well, how can you be excited about work? I'm not excited about the work. I'm excited about the outcome, the results, and what it does for others.

I'm passionate about uplifting and empowering others through multiple methods. Through our work models, through our training programs, through what we provide to our clients, to our customers. I'm excited about it. Hopefully that shows through. I want my team to be inspired and get excited about what they can do and how they can contribute to that and how they can make that happen. It's contagious. Express genuine enthusiasm. Share your passions and share your interests naturally in your conversation. Practice empathy. Be empathetic of others, building that trust and that likability around you. Put yourself in other's shoes. How are they feeling? How would that make them feel? How are they reacting? How are they responding? What do you see coming from them? Then consistent positivity. Even in the face of a challenge. We all have our days where we wake up on the wrong side of the bed. I would start focusing on and analyze what can be done to turn this around. How can I leverage this and use it to my benefit? What can I take away from this? What did I learn? Extract anything that was useful out of the situation. That positive attitude is going to attract people and create that atmosphere around you that pulls people in. That makes you magnetic. That lights up the room, that energy. People like that positive energy. Why? Because they can feed off it. It's contagious. They feel inspired, motivated, and uplifted. Who wants to go to something and be around people that are, oh, well, another thing went wrong. Nobody wants to be around that. They want to be around inspiration. They want to feel uplifted. Give that to them. Have a positive outlook and focus on the solutions rather than the problem or the challenge. Focus on what came from it. Focus on what you learned from it. Get excited about the fact that you learned something new to add in to your valuable knowledge you already have. Adaptability. Being able to adapt your communication style to different people and different situations is key. It's a key aspect of charisma. Observe what's going on around you. Focus on the surrounding people. Then adjust your communication style and preferences of the people that you're around and that you're interacting with. Charisma and influence are powerful tools in business. If you have that energy, magnetism, and charisma, you will attract more people.

How do we gain more business? We introduce ourselves to more people more often. We also want to have that charisma in our sales process, in our marketing, in what our brand's known for. In brand authority, in your PR, in your customer interactions, in your team. You want that motivation, that inspiring feeling, throughout your team. This is a powerful tool. If you can work on these little tips and start implementing them into your daily routine, into your business, you're going to inspire teams. You're going to win clients. You're going to lead effectively. People say, "Christy, if I'm feeling down for the day, that's not authentic." What you choose to show is a choice, who you are in that moment, and what you convey. You're not changing who you are. You're not changing your core. That's still there in the center of things, your values, who you are, what makes you unique. That's still there. You're just turning around your core. You're turning to express what's needed in that moment. That's called leadership. You don't always feel you have all the energy in the world. I don't always feel like this is a wonderful thing that we just had this huge roadblock that popped up. Of course, we don't feel that way. But that positive outlook, being positive in a negative situation, this is one of my favorite quotes. Ralph Marston said, “Remaining positive in a negative situation is not being naïve. It's called leadership.” I love that quote. It's so true. To be a genuine leader, a leader in business, a leader to your teams, in your community, within your client base, and among competitors. Have that energy, that passion, that positive outlook on everything you do. Turn it around. You have the power to do that. It's your choice. It's so important if you want to scale your business quickly. I want you to remember walking away from this chapter that charisma is not about being the most outgoing or flamboyant person in the room. That's not what it is. It's about connecting with people genuinely and understanding those people, empathizing with those people, and making them feel valued. Charisma, having that oomph, that spark, being magnetic, lighting up a room, being the energy in the room, is never about you. It's not about your personality. It's not about what you can do. It's always about others and what you do for them. How do you make them feel? That's charisma.

Effective communication starts with asking open-ended questions that invite detailed responses. Show genuine interest by asking things like, “How did that make you feel?” or “What do you think would be the best outcome?” Avoid yes/no questions—give people space to share their thoughts. Also, pay attention to nonverbal cues like body language and tone of voice. Subtly mirror the speaker’s body language (without copying exactly) to build rapport. People naturally connect with those who reflect their own behaviors.

An additional one is perspective taking. Actively put yourself in the other person's shoes as they're speaking. Imagine how you would have felt in that situation to gain insight into their emotions. Then empathy mapping. Empathy mapping is a tool to understand others better. It involves truly considering what others are seeing, hearing, thinking, and feeling. Putting yourself in their shoes a little deeper, really mapping that out to understand what they're going through. That leads to validating feelings. Acknowledge and validate the other person's feelings. Even if you don't agree with their perspective, that's okay. Different perspectives are great in that we don't all have to agree. That's the beauty of it. Take the same topic and have thousands of perspectives on that topic. That is what's fantastic about learning from each other and being able to collaborate and having a diverse group of opinions. You don't have to agree with everyone, but you can acknowledge and validate the other person's feelings. For example, even if you don't agree with what they're saying, you can absolutely say, *I understand that this is important to you.* Or *I can see that this has upset you and I understand where you're coming from*. Or *I understand why that would have been so important to you in that situation*. Acknowledge what they said. *I'm hearing everything you're saying about X, Y, Z. I can see why you'd feel that way*. Affirm what they're feeling. They just want someone to hear and validate.

Another one is emotional literacy. Improve your ability to identify and name emotions accurately in yourself and in others. Practice recognizing that wide range of emotional states beyond basic emotions. You really want to dig deep and identify the underlying emotion when somebody's speaking. It takes practice, but you will get better at it, and it will come naturally. Another thing is cultivating curiosity about others. Cultivate a genuine interest in people with different backgrounds and different experiences. You want that diversity. You're going to learn from it. You're going to listen to other perspectives and gain so much, so many valuable insights from that. Engage with diverse groups of people in different industries. It doesn't have to be your industry, competitors, non-competitors, people that do something completely different, different geographic areas. Broaden your understanding of various perspectives. You don't want to keep to the same little group as you'll learn those emotions and you'll learn those habits, but you're not going to really practice and get a good understanding or a good way of feeling out a wide range of emotions and feelings. Another thing is to practice empathy in daily interactions. Regular practice of empathy in everyday situations, whether that's with your friends, your family, or at work. You don't want to do it just in high stakes or emotional situations, but in normal conversation. Practice it. It'll become a habit, and then you can use that in emotional conversations or high stakes discussions. Finally, self-reflection. Reflect on those interactions that you've had and consider how you could have been even more empathetic. How could you do it better? Just like you look at your business and say, how can we improve? How can I improve on how I listen? How can I improve on how I empathize with someone? Think about situations from the past. Don't dwell on the past, live in the present, but think about some situations from the past and how empathy may have changed the outcome had you listened or responded differently, had you really understood the individual's motivation for the behavior. Another thing we talked about was effective communication. That's a big part of charisma.

A top tip for effective communication is clear and concise messaging. Keep your message clear and to the point. Avoid a bunch of unnecessary jargon or overly complex language. Use simple language that's easily understood by your audience. You want the entire audience to take away as much as possible and you don't want to over-complicate something. A lot of times the reason the message doesn't resonate, it's not memorable. People don't walk away feeling inspired or take something big away from it is because it was over-complicated. Make it easy and use direct language. That's something they can take away, easily break down, process, and understand. Another big thing for effective communication is active listening. I know we've covered this with empathy and other things, but practice active listening by focusing entirely on the person speaking. Nodding, eye contact, affirmative sounds, or words. Don't interrupt, don't speak to take over, don't listen to speak, but listen to understand while validating, acknowledging, and showing that you're listening and interested in what they're saying.

One thing that we cover is having your voice flow smoothly. It shouldn't be broken up and hard to follow. It should be a flow. That also includes elevating your voice sometimes when you're grabbing attention, making it a little softer to draw people in, come a little closer, listen to this, it's a secret. When you're excited, you might have a bit of volume adjustment. Another thing is the rate of speech. You don't want to speak so quickly that you've lost your audience, but sometimes it's good to speed up. Then when there's something that you really want them to take away. That's where you slow it down and your body language will match. You want to increase and decrease that rate of speech, making it a nice flowy conversation, something that keeps people's attention. It reactivates the attention piece of their brain. It says, hey, over here again, to re-engage them. If you're speaking at the same even tone and the same even pace throughout, guess what? Your audience is zoned out. Hang on a word that you really want to emphasize. There are different ways to do that. Practice that in your everyday speaking.

We're going back to body language. Take it back to body language. Those open gestures, maintaining your eye contact, your facial expression should match your words. It should be authentic and engaging. Observe also the nonverbal cues of others when you're speaking to better understand their emotion, how they're connecting, how your message is resonating with them. Read how that person's responding. If they're bored and looking away, and if they're looking up, if they're thinking about something else, your message is not resonating. You're not saying something that's important or of value to them. Look at the verbal cues of your audience while you're speaking, and then pivot and adjust your methods or adjust what you're going to do or say next to tailor it to what your audience needs in the moment. Practice that in your everyday conversation, and when you practice it there, you're going to translate that over to a work presentation, a client meeting, a speaking event, or whatever it might be.

Another big one is empathy in responding. Show empathy by acknowledging the other person's perspective and emotions. You can use phrases like, *I understand how that might frustrate*, or *wow, I see this is very important to you*, or *wow, from what you're saying, I've gathered that...and* then fill in the blank. Implement a feedback loop in your communication. Restate or summarize what you've learned to ensure that you're understanding correctly and show the individual that you were listening, and you're concerned about ensuring you know exactly what they were conveying. In an interactive situation where I'm training live, I solicit feedback throughout my presentation. When I'm presenting to a client, I pause at different pieces and ask for their perspective on something. Well, what are they thinking? Tell me a bit about what you're looking to see here. Invite them in. Effective pausing and pacing, but use pauses effectively to give emphasis to your points. It also allows time for the listener to process information. In a speaking event or a training, sometimes it's good to take a breather or to pause. When you don't know what you're going to say next, it's okay to take a couple of seconds to pause and regroup with your thoughts and give the audience time to process what you've been saying. Pausing before responding gives you that time also to plan your next thought and make sure that it's effective.

Your tone of voice. Are you speaking about something where it's exciting and you should have that excitement conveyed? Are you speaking to someone about a serious situation? In that case, you want to be very mindful of your tone and it should be appropriate to the context and content of that conversation. Adjust based on what you're talking about and who you're speaking with. A friendly and positive tone will lead to a more receptive audience, even if it's a tough conversation, even if you find yourself amid a mini conflict, that positive tone can lead to a more receptive conversation. Another thing is to be approachable and open-minded. You don't want to go in with this thought of, I'm set on this, and this is the end all be all. You don't want to do that. Maintain an open-minded and approachable demeanor. You want to listen to new ideas, hear different perspectives, and not just listen, but consider them and integrate that into the conversation and plan. It fosters an environment where open and honest communication is encouraged and whether that's between customers, your team members, other people around you at a networking event, a speaking event, or at work, it doesn't matter. Then, the last piece in here is to practice your public speaking and presentation skills. Regular practice in public speaking can significantly enhance your overall communication skills. You can practice in front of a mirror. Sometimes just practicing a one-minute thing in front of a mirror can help you feel more confident. It can help to reveal areas you may want to work on. You may want to adjust your tone, the pace, your posture, or your body language. Focus on clarity, engagement, and confidence when you're speaking, because that's going to translate over to a larger group of people.

Finally, it brings us to the last tool in this toolkit, which is being authentic. I know we started by saying, "But Christy, doesn't this contradict?" No. To identify what makes you authentic, you want to reflect on your values, beliefs, principles, and your why. What do you stand for? What are your passions? What do you dislike? You could talk your way through it in front of a mirror. You could just talk it over in your head or with somebody else, a trusted friend, a colleague, a leadership buddy, or another business owner. Reflect on what makes you who you are. What makes you unique? Be true to your values. Even though I will adjust my presentation, my method of delivery, my tone of voice, the context, or the content, one thing I do not adjust are my values. Once you understand your values, you want to ensure your actions and words align with those. That's how you're going to come across as your authentic self. Be consistent in what you say and do. Your actions reinforce authenticity. If you're saying this, but you're doing that, you're inconsistent. That does not convey that authentic self that you want to convey. You should regularly review your decisions and actions and ensure that they align with your core values. It's important to do that self-reflection frequently. Another thing is to communicate honestly. Authenticity involves honest and transparent communication. It's about expressing those true thoughts and feelings, but in a respectful and constructive manner, whether it's with your team, customers, or with coworkers, it doesn't matter. Be honest and transparent in what you do and how you do business. Practice clear and open communication. Don't be afraid to show vulnerability where it's appropriate. You can still come across as confident. You can come across as assertive, but vulnerable.

Another thing is you want to accept your strengths and weaknesses. Being authentic means acknowledging strengths and flaws. No one is perfect. If you come across as perfect, people are going to know it's not authentic. Admitting the areas that you struggle in or admitting challenges, especially if you've been able to overcome some of them, can help somebody else and it can empower you and others that you're looking to motivate and inspire. It is important to accept both your strengths and your weaknesses.

And listen to feedback. Authenticity involves being open to feedback. Even when it's critical, when you don't want to hear it. Try not to become defensive, or you go into that mode of justification. Feedback helps you grow and stay grounded. Seek feedback from customers, team members, family members, and friends, and reflect on it honestly. Ask yourself, is there truth to this? Reflect on that and then make changes as necessary. Avoid comparisons. Being authentic means being you. It means being Christy, and I can't mess that up. Christy is who Christy is, and that's the one thing that she does perfectly. Don't measure up to someone else. It's okay to have mentors, goals, and role models. Those are all good things, but put your own spin on it. Be yourself while listening to advice or watching somebody and say, I really like that piece. I want to implement that, but put your own spin on it. Don't measure up. It leads to inauthentic behavior. Focus on being the best version of yourself. Remind yourself of all your unique qualities.

Finally, practicing what you preach. Authenticity is going to be shown through your actions more so than your words. Yes, you want to be consistent in your communication verbally, but you also want to be consistent in demonstrating the actions that align with your values.

Ensure that your behavior matches those spoken principles and regularly assess whether your actions reflect your spoken commitments. That's whether it's in business or life. Make that a practice. You're going to build so much more rapport and an authentic brand that really resonates with your ideal customer if you use your authenticity to build that rapport. Share your genuine opinions, show interest in others, and be present in conversations. Recognize and appreciate the authenticity in others just as you should in yourself. This mutual recognition will strengthen your business relationships, whether that's your team, your customers, networking opportunities, or your peers.

The biggest take away, charisma, is a set of practiced behaviors and skills. You can practice them daily in your routines, and you can become that magnetic energy in the room, that speaker that's so dynamic that people want to go see. They give off that energy. They're the person who lights up the room. You know who I'm talking about? That can be you. It is you. It's in there. You just have to dig down and really practice revealing that while still maintaining your authenticity. Practice it in the mirror, with family, at the grocery store, at work, or in your everyday life. Do it a bit in every conversation and then see how you feel after a week and see how that has become a natural behavior.

The Psychology Behind Persuasion

We're going to cover the psychology behind persuasion. Understanding it is fascinating and crucial in both your personal and professional spheres. We will break down some key psychological principles of persuasion, and that will provide you with some practical, easy-to-apply tips within your business. For this book, we want to focus on the key principles that influence decision-making. This is going to be important within your sales department, your leadership team, and any of your marketing and advertising materials with your clients, potential clients, vendors, even when you're negotiating contracts and pricing. Understanding what influences people's decisions is very important in being able to tailor your approach effectively.

The first key point we want to talk about is reciprocity, giving first. People have a natural tendency to reciprocate gestures or favors. Think about it. Has someone done something for you? What is typically the feeling around that? That you can easily give something back to them. Or you owe them a favor. Now, I'm not saying we should use this for the wrong purpose. When I give to someone, I give because I'm giving. I've decided to give. I like to make it about others. I don't like to use it, but it's good to understand this principle. It means that we can offer valuable advice, free samples, or helpful information and set the stage for that tendency to reciprocate. It doesn't mean that they owe us. It doesn't mean we expect it, but by providing a lot of value, something helpful, or free items, it sets them up to really feel like it's okay to share something back with us. That's how we should look at it. That's something important to understand. The next thing is going to be commitment and consistency. The power of small steps. People uphold commitments to maintain consistency in their actions. Start with small steps or gain little agreements on things before proposing a larger partnership, commitment, or offer. Start with small requests. As you're talking with someone, you want to seek that buy-in as you're going through the process. It can be a buy in, and can we agree on that? Or do you agree with that? Or would that be okay? Or I'd like to share the study with you and the results that this client saw. Would that be all right to do? You're getting little buy ins, little agreements. Or ask them for something early in a sales process. Could I ask you for your sales figures? Could I ask you for your goal in 2024? Start with those small requests, ask for little things, little commitments, gain that buy-in as you're going through.

This also works when we're talking with your team. Gain that buy-in, gain that commitment in little steps as you're going through leading up to a bigger project. Can we all agree to commit to XYZ? Or John, do I have your commitment to deliver XYZ? Make it small and then increase it as you move through that process. Another psychological principle is social proof. Leverage the power of influence. People naturally seek validation from the actions and decisions of others. Use true testimonials from your customers. Use examples. You can use social media endorsements, influencers, people that will promote your brand for you. You always want to present the result. Think about your ideal audience. What keeps them up at night? Then present the answer.

For example, you will not go to a chiropractor's office and tell them I'm going to sell you marketing services or sales services. No, you want to think about what is that chiropractor looking for. They're looking for more patients. More patients, more revenue, more patients lead to more revenue. What are you going to sell them? *Oh, hey Dr. John, I can guarantee you at least 10 new patients a month* or *Dr. John, let's get you four new patients a week*. Sell the result. Show your ideal audience proof of that, proof of what you can do. Show the endorsement, the testimony, the reviews, show that it's worked for other people. People look at that and, in their mind, they validate and say, *well, it worked for them. It could work for me. It worked for John chiropractor over here. It could work for me.* You want to show the acceptance and popularity of your idea, your brand, your product, and your service.

Moving on, establishing credibility and influence. People are much more likely to be persuaded by credible and knowledgeable authorities. Share your experience, credentials, and knowledge to establish that authority in your field. It's going to set you apart from your competitors. This does not mean you have to be arrogant. It means that you show what you're doing. For example, in my organization, Next Level Connected digital marketing, I show my experience. I get permission from clients and say, "For example, a chiropractor, we increased their revenue by 30% in the first four months. Let me show you the proof. Let me show you what we've done." Or "I spoke on the same topic at this summit," or "I trained the state of Alabama on the same topic at XYZ," or "I trained this division within the state of Florida be able to achieve X results." Those are things that I have done. Or use some of your media examples, your expertise, things that you were featured in, establish that credibility, establish the fact that you are an expert at what you do. This differentiates you from your competitors.

Next key point, building connections, liking, similarity. People like and connect with what they feel like. How do you build rapport? Well, you find a common ground; you find something shared, and that similarity increases the likelihood of persuasion. It also immediately builds rapport. People are drawn to similarities. We talk about how to mirror somebody's actions, behaviors, word structure, flow, and emotions because people are drawn to similarities. You can build rapport by finding those common interests and showing an interest in them. Build a connection before you persuade, make sure you connect, bond with that person, show where you're similar and where you're relatable. Establish that connection first before looking to persuade them. Next key point in persuasion and decision-making, exclusivity. You create value through scarcity. Now, that does not mean we have to be deceitful and say we only have three available, but a perceived scarcity increases the perceived value of an offer or opportunity. Emphasize why it is unique. You don't want to sell something better. Sell something different, but in a good way. You want limited availability. Making that decision, make them feel like a VIP. This is time sensitive. They should act now. This is exclusive for this VIP group. When you're selling, you can often focus on what their expertise is. Remember, we talked about focusing on others. Focus on, I'm finding that doctors who are very intelligent who have definitely scaled past this are seeing XYZ, or this program is really geared toward people who are an expert in this. It sells to that feeling of a VIP group, exclusivity. You can really emphasize what differentiates your product, service, brand, and yourself, and really focus on those features to create that value. Those are some of the key points to note when we're talking about persuasion and influence in decision-making. This isn't just for sales. I know we talk a lot about this applying to sales presentations and pitches and potential clients, but this can also be applied to decision-making within your teams or your vendors when you're negotiating contracts and prices for products or services. You can use this in many areas when you're connecting with others.

Techniques for Captivating Audiences

We're going to focus on techniques for captivating audiences. You do not have to be a frequent speaker or get up in front of large groups. This can also apply to small group settings, networking events, your team, or small groups of clients. Work on captivating an audience. This does not have to be some big speaking event. We're going to talk about some key elements to ensure that your message not only captures their attention but keeps it. A lot of these techniques will sound familiar. Remember, we talked about crafting a compelling and memorable message. The number one thing when considering the creation of a message that resonates is to know your audience. You're going to see that's a recurring theme in many things that you're going to need in your business. If you don't know who you're speaking to, you absolutely cannot capture their attention. It's the same thing when you're selling. If you don't know who you're selling to, you will not be very effective at selling.

First, know your audience. Tailor your content to their interests, their needs, and their level of understanding. Do your research. Second, you want to begin your presentation with a surprising fact, thought-provoking question, or a compelling story. Use an analogy, an antidote, a statistic that's related to your topic. Make sure it's relative and will resonate with your audience to grab their attention. We talk about hooks on social media. You have the first 10 seconds to hook your audience in. They're going to size things up and determine, are they going to be engaged in this conversation? Now, that's not to say you can't draw them in if the first technique didn't work, but really those first 10 seconds are the impression you make. That's where they're going to say, *let me pay attention to this person. I want to join in this conversation.* Third, variety in delivery. Vary your tone, your pace, and your volume. That does not mean scream at somebody. It does not mean go so fast that they can't keep up. It means that there should be variety and flow within your conversation. When you're having a conversation with someone, you want it to feel natural. That means there's going to be a varied tone. Sometimes you're going to emphasize specific words. You're going to slow your speech to emphasize. You're going to speed up in other areas. You're going to change your volume when you're talking about something exciting. When you're talking about something else, you might take your volume down a notch. When you want to draw them in, you might reduce your volume to help the brain maintain interest. Monotony is the enemy of audience engagement. A tip on that one is to practice in front of a mirror before you go to speak. Try different vocal variations to find what works for you and what works for your audience. Remember, number one is to know your audience.

Engage your audience with interactive elements. If it's a virtual setting, incorporate tools like Q&A Sessions or polls. In-person, encourage audience participation to create a two-way dialogue. Visuals can also help, but they should complement, not dominate, your message. Whether using slides, videos, or charts, keep them as a background aid. You don't want your audience reading off the screen—you want them paying attention to you.

Effective body language is key. Whether standing, sitting, or moving, how you position yourself on stage—or even in front of a webcam—matters. Your body should help your audience feel your message. Confident body language—open, inviting gestures, purposeful movement—shows you're in control. If you're stationary, that's fine too, but still use your arms, hands, and facial expressions to convey energy. Practice in front of a mirror or record yourself to observe any closed-off gestures. Always face your audience, keep your body engaged, and use your eyes and expressions to share your emotions.

Next, let's talk about storytelling. Relatable stories are a powerful way to captivate. Whether it's a personal anecdote, a client's journey, or even a TV show you saw—make sure the story ties directly to your topic. Authenticity is crucial. Share stories that reveal something personal about you or those you've worked with. This creates a deeper connection with your audience and leads to an emotional bond. Stories that evoke emotions are more likely to be remembered. Aim to tug at those heart strings. Keep them on the edge of their seat. If you were anxious during that period or they're waiting on the edge of their seat to hear how this resolved, they're concerned, excited, motivated, inspired, or whatever emotion you're conveying, make sure it's within your story. A good thing to do is to include challenges to overcome or moments of revelation within the story. How did it feel? The light bulb went on. Tell that piece of the story. You also want to have a logical structure for your story. We talked about the rule of three. Have a clear beginning, middle, and an end. Structure your story so it leads the audience through a journey. Plan your story with a bang, set up, beginning. Some confrontation, challenge is your middle. That's the peak. I'm at the edge of my seat. Then your resolution is your end, your solution, whatever it might be. Add in visual descriptions. Use descriptive language to create those vivid images in the minds of your audience. Paint the picture for them. That's going to engage them in whatever you're talking about. Paint a specific and vivid image that's going to be more memorable. You can include sensory details. Finally, you want to make sure that story links back to your message. You want it to align with your overall message, whatever that is. Then conclude your story by linking it back to the main point of your presentation or tie it back in. You don't want to just tell a story to tell a story.

If it doesn't relate back to what you're talking about, the audience is sitting there confused and being distracted from the main point. They're sitting there trying to make sense of the story you told. What does that have to do with engaging content to captivate an audience? It doesn't. Leave it out if it doesn't align. Really capturing the attention of your audience and holding it requires a blend of strategic content delivery and the art of storytelling. Something memorable, tying it in, relating it to things that make sense to them, things that are in their everyday life, a story that they can jump inside of and remember and take that piece away with them. Encourage them to connect with you emotionally when you're speaking. You can practice some of these techniques by putting together a quick presentation for something you can use for a client. Add a bit of storytelling in. Practice in front of a mirror and watch your body language, your facial expressions, how you deliver that message to see if that's what you're conveying. Practice, and if you implement these tips, you're going to see it become natural. You're going to get up there on stage, get in front of a group of people and you're going to see it naturally flow out, because it becomes muscle memory, habit.

Conclusion Decoding People Dynamics

Let's talk about how everything we've discussed within this chapter of decoding people dynamics ties into your business growth. You're here to shatter through the seven-figure, eight-figure ceiling, wherever you are on your business journey. Whether you're starting out, in the middle, or already making eight figures and you're looking to go to nine figures or the next mark. How does this tie in? Why did we go over all of this?

Let's talk about active listening. That was woven in throughout a lot of this chapter. Well, we're going to use active listening during every piece of our business, during customer interactions. We want to make sure that we understand the needs and preferences of our customers so that we can create a tailored product, service, or solution that increases customer satisfaction and loyalty from our customers. Understanding how to truly listen to understand, not to listen to form a response, and how to be empathetic in our listening. It's going to shape our solutions and how they differ from our competitors, setting us apart. It's also going to come into play when we're talking about building teams. As you scale, you will need teams, or outsourced help and resources.

You are going to need to deal with conflict resolution, to motivate them, understand their decision-making processes, and understand their motivation to build a world-class team. What drives them, how are they affected by different things, what are their emotions, what are their feelings? Why do you need a world-class team? If you don't have the best people, you will not have the best products and services. They make or break your business. You might be starting out and you're like, oh, don't worry about it. I'm a solopreneur. I got this. If you want to scale past seven, eight, nine figures, you're eventually going to need to have a team or surround yourself with resources. To do that, you're going to need to master active listening. When I say master, I mean, get fantastic at it. We want to have a constant growth mindset. Always be open to learning a better technique or to do better to continue to grow and learn.

Let's talk about effective communication a bit. This is going to play into every part of business growth. But let's think about marketing for a moment. You need to have clear and persuasive communication within your marketing strategies, convey your value proposition effectively, increase your brand awareness, and therefore your sales. Because people buy from people, from brands they trust, because it solves a problem. You need to create a marketing message that directly addresses pain points and solves the challenge, the pain point, whatever it is. You want it to solve, to heal the problem. Know exactly what they want and be able to communicate how your solution takes care of that. You need effective communication there. Empathetic leadership is so important within your team. You might say, "Christy, I'm just starting out. I don't have a team yet." That's okay, but you will. If it's not your team, empathetic leadership within your business, setting you apart from competitors, leading among the sea of other services and products that are like your own. Empathy and emotional intelligence are important here. We want to understand and address team member and customer concerns. This will lead to improved morale within your team, better teamwork, and increased productivity. It leads to better solutions for your customers when we solicit their feedback and we put ourselves in their shoes to truly understand what it is they want, what's working, what's not working. We talked a lot about storytelling. Why is this important? It's important, especially for branding and sales. Incorporate that storytelling into your branding, your sales strategy, a story about your brand's journey, about your personal journey, customer success stories, results for clients. It can enhance an emotional connection and therefore trust, and people buy from people they trust. You want that for your marketing, your sales, and your branding.

We went over a couple of key points briefly for psychology and persuasion techniques, for negotiations. This doesn't even have to be sales negotiations. It can be, but negotiations with vendors. Getting a better price, creating a partnership, apply persuasion techniques in these negotiations to achieve more favorable terms for yourself. This can be suppliers, partners, or in sales. Use things like exclusivity. Keep it in the forefront of your mind. Social proof works to drive sales. This will help you strengthen your position and help you to custom tailor your approach to whatever it is, negotiating that contract, closing that sales deal. When we talk about conflict resolution, this might come into play for customer service within your brand, your teams, vendors, or a client. This can apply to many areas. Work on resolving conflicts promptly and constructively. Putting yourself in their shoes to understand why they're responding the way they are, understanding how they're going to respond, envisioning what emotion that's going to drive and, therefore, how they're going to react to whatever it is you're presenting. Also, de-escalation skills and being able to read people. Noting a shift in behavior, in demeanor, in tone, in what they're saying, a change in their body language, can help you better target your message to convey it and prep that individual or adjust your style, your presentation method, or your approach based on their reactions. This is for clients, vendors, team members, every individual you encounter within your business.

I have found that growing my business is contingent upon using these skills. This is how you grow your business. This is how you scale quickly. It is a huge foundation for shattering that seven or eight-figure ceiling. There are real tangible applications in growing your business. If you apply these skills in areas like customer interactions, team management, marketing, and negotiations, you're going to see a significant impact on sales, team dynamics, and customer satisfaction. Start implementing these tips daily, practice them in front of the mirror, with your friends and family, out when meeting strangers, at the grocery store, in a networking environment, or at work. Then you're going to observe transformation in business outcomes based on using these tips effectively. Remember how to maintain that and then continue to grow to the next level. We want to strive toward constant growth, and we don't just want to hit seven figures this year. No, no, no. We want to hit seven figures consistently, maintain that and then set our goal for eight figures. We want to create sustainable growth within our businesses. These keys to decoding people dynamics and understanding how people think, how they work, how to custom tailor your approach, products, services, marketing, sales, and every aspect of your business is going to help you with that sustainable growth in your business.

The next chapter is going to focus on networking. If you've ever felt like networking is a maze of awkward conversations, missed opportunities, waste of your time, I want you to prepare an open mind of how we're going to turn that around because mastering networking like a pro for business success is a chapter that will transform you into a networking superstar. I hear a lot from business owners. I don't have time for networking. I've got to get into my business. I've got to make these sales. Networking means more sales. Networking is the key to growing and scaling a business. We're going to dive into strategies that top business leaders use to build influential connections, to uncover hidden opportunities that might be missed, and create lasting professional relationships that are going to benefit you, not just from a sales aspect, but also from a growth aspect, a learning aspect, and partnership aspects to tremendous opportunities to leverage your brand. We're talking about conferences, community events, and online networking platforms, navigating scenarios with confidence and ease.

Remember, confidence is a choice. I've said it 15 times, at least, but repeat it to yourself in the mirror. Confidence, charisma, it's a choice. It's a set of behaviors. How do we uncover that within ourselves? It's sitting in all of us. Practice. We're going to apply those concepts in the networking world and talk about specifics that align with meeting new people and expanding our networks to benefit the growth of our business. We'll talk about first impressions, fostering valuable connections that go beyond just handing out a business card. That's not networking. Handing out a business card and walking away is not networking. We're going to go through insider tips I use and that I train my clients to use in practical application settings. We're going to leave behind those days of ineffective networking, throwing out some business cards. It's time to step into the world of strategic, meaningful, and result-oriented networking that's going to propel your business forward.

Quick Networking Tips for Business Owners Short on Time

Short on time but need to network to grow your business. This quick guide offers smart, efficient strategies for busy entrepreneurs and business owners to build valuable connections. From making networking a daily habit to leveraging social media, these tips will help you network effectively without taking too much time from your busy schedule. Perfect for those who want to grow their network and their business profits!

http://bit.ly/4gkLcHz

Chapter 5 Mastering Networking for Business Success

We're going to cover mastering networking for business success. This chapter transforms your professional interactions and turns them into incredible opportunities. I'll be guiding you through the art of networking, not just as a business skill, but as a personal growth skill for connection. It brings success, in business and in life. Imagine if you could join a group, knowing exactly how to engage, who to connect with, and how to leave a lasting impression with everyone you meet. It's not just a skill, it's an art. An art that has propelled countless professionals to the peaks of their career. Behind every successful business story, there's a network of connections and relationships that play a crucial role in their business growth. In my journey, I've seen firsthand how a single conversation can open doors and opportunities that I never imagined.

I met a fellow entrepreneur at a conference. It was just a random encounter. We turned that into a fantastic partnership with a large conglomerate that drove both of our businesses to new successes. They're not just interactions. They're seeds you're planting for your future. Most business owners miss this piece. They miss the connection of networking. *I don't have time for it. I don't know how to do that. That's not for me. I just do the business part.* This is the business part. Everything from an unforgettable introduction, making you memorable, to nurturing professional relationships. We're going to explore strategies used by other top business leaders, how they approach networking events, manage professional relationships, and leverage these connections for growth. We're going to explore the tools and confidence to network like a pro. Whether you're just starting out or you're a seasoned business professional, or somewhere in between, we're going to touch on these points and make you a master networking pro.

Confident Networking Strategies for Success

Let's jump right into networking. People think of it as a place you exchange business cards. Networking is more than that. It's meant to build relationships and create a lasting impression. It's a great way to open doors to opportunities. We're going to really enhance your networking confidence and your success in connecting with new people.

Starting out, let's go over some basics of networking. The first thing you really want to do when you're planning networking events, online, at a speaking event, a conference, a summit, is to develop a clear networking goal. Ask yourself, what am I aiming to achieve through this networking? Is it finding potential clients or a mentor at this event? Is it making industry or vendor connections? Is it all three? I tell people that when you're networking, try not to go in with the sole purpose of I'm looking to sell my products, because that's what you convey.

When I go into a networking event, I look at it as this is exciting, who can I meet? What can I offer them? How can I connect with people? When you shift the focus to what you can do for others and how you can connect, you're going to come across as authentic. You're going to make genuine connections. The significant side effect of that is that often it leads to opportunities. Not a direct sale, a direct customer, a direct vendor relationship, but an introduction to the right person. It only takes one introduction, to create a chain effect of meeting the right people. Before you go to the networking event, sometimes the goal is to sell to clients if that's what that event is set up to do. But I would not set that as your primary goal. I would set the goal as what can I do to connect?

Entering Conversations with Ease

Once you've set your networking goal, the next step is to craft a memorable introduction. Think of your introduction as a way to immediately grab someone's attention by addressing their ultimate desire or problem. Keep your elevator pitch short and impactful—less than 30 seconds. People have short attention spans, so you need to capture their interest within the first 10 seconds. Avoid lengthy introductions filled with fluff. Instead, clearly state what you do and how you help others. Rather than making it all about you, transition the conversation into something engaging and centered on the other person. The goal is to connect, not just inform. Once you've delivered your quick pitch, turn the focus toward the person you're speaking with and engage in a two-way conversation. Networking is about creating an authentic connection, not just listing your accolades. By centering the conversation around the other person, you become more memorable and approachable. You want to practice your pitch. Other coaches in the industry will tell you that you can just memorize this elevator pitch and use it wherever you go. Here's specifically what you specialize in, and that's it. Deliver it. I completely disagree. I disagree with having one elevator pitch that just says it all. I disagree with going past 30 seconds on an elevator pitch. You should deliver exactly how you're going to solve all their problems or how you're going to deliver their ultimate desire in those first 10 seconds, along with your name. The rest should be just a little teaser or tidbit about how you do that or what it is you do from there. There's your profession. There's your specialty. There's where you insert that. Then the conversation should be turned to that person.

You're saying, "Christy, what do you mean? Your elevator pitch is who you are." No, *your elevator pitch is what you do for others.* We must shift our thought process to make the focus to other person centric. That means making others the center of what you do. Your elevator pitch should not talk about your accolades and all your awards and achievements. No. Something that grabs attention and is going to stand out and be memorable is giving your name and exactly what you do to deliver the solution or solve their problem. That is your elevator pitch. Then a little tidbit about the teaser of how. I know that's controversial. They will tell you to use the same elevator pitch. Absolutely not.

What you want to do, the trick to delivering a memorable and attention-grabbing elevator pitch is to get the other individual to introduce themselves first. You take that moment to learn who they are. What would their pain point be? What would their desire be? What do they want ultimately? Then I adjust or pivot in my elevator pitch to tailor it to that specific person. Now, that does not mean I make things up. All I do is tailor what I specialize in, what I do to what can I do for them, if it's something I can do for them, and I just give it to them right there to grab their attention. Right then, you can get into a two-way conversation. You should not be memorizing a 30-second script and just delivering it to everybody you meet. Your elevator pitch, who you are, should be what you do for that other person. It should be custom-tailored to each individual that you meet at a networking event. That's how to get the most out of that event. That's how to meet more people. That's how to become memorable. That's how to communicate exactly what it is you do and who you are. Make it about the other person.

We will create a great elevator pitch. You can also reach out after this, and we can walk through some tips, suggestions of what it is. I'm going to give you some examples of what I've used and what you can use. Practice your pitch. You don't want to practice one 30-second script. Practice the overall goal of your pitch. That's why you want to know your audience before you go to a networking event. Then you just adjust it, tweak it slightly for each individual that you meet. Don't just dump information. Don't deliver a 30-second script of this is all about me. Reflect your personality, your passion. How you deliver your elevator pitch is just as important as what you say. Somebody who has your own unique energy, enthusiasm, personality, and passion, if that shines through, that's going to be memorable as well. Deliver it the right way and then provide them with, I'm so-and-so. Who does this? It should be the solution or the delivery of exactly what they want. Then a little tidbit about how interesting, in a teasing manner. It means tease so that you can then continue that conversation. Or if they're interested, they'll let you know, and you'll continue down that road.

When you start a conversation, don't dump information right away. First, ask the other person to introduce themselves.

Next, be mindful of your body language. Keep your stance open—avoid crossing your arms, which can make you look unapproachable. Eye contact is key, and even if it's hard for you, it's important to try. A smile can be incredibly powerful, as it instantly makes you more inviting and approachable. Smiles create a connection that draws people in.

Practice some of those body language expressions. Do it in front of a mirror. Before you go, practice. Start talking to yourself in the mirror and then ask, is that the person I would like to approach at a networking event, or engage in a meaningful conversation with? Is that somebody interesting? Would that body language attract me to that individual? I know we're all our own worst critics. But look at it objectively from your facial expressions, body language, gestures, eye contact, smiling with your eyes and mouth, and your face. Conveying that open, inviting behavior, how to create that magnetism, have your passion shine through. If you don't want to look in the mirror, record yourself, play it back, and then see how you want to adjust that when you go to the event.

Next, we talked a lot about active listening being a key. That's how we learn about the other person, audience, or the group we're in front of. Active listening is how you assess exactly what you need to deliver to introduce yourself. I like to think of it as we're multifaceted people. We're showing exactly that piece of us. It's still a piece of us. Your authentic self is your core values. You don't change those or your personality. But you might mirror other people's behaviors or tone to make them feel more comfortable. Remember, it's all about them. Focus on the other person, group, or the person speaking. Then ask questions, open-ended, relevant questions. People like to talk about themselves. When you allow them that opportunity, it's going to give you the chance to learn about them and be able to respond meaningfully, memorably, in a way that's going to create the connection you need to form that relationship. Follow-up in networking is crucial. After you meet someone, follow-up with a personalized message after the event, summit, or speaking event, even if it's a virtual event. This helps solidify that connection. Remember them and show that they were important to you. Mention something specific from your conversation that you had, something you learned, talked about; or connected over. When you follow up and you are remembering what it is you discussed, you're showing that your conversation was valuable to you. They were not just another person on the list that you touched base with, you connected.

Next, a big thing about networking in today's digital age is going to be leveraging social media platforms. I know a lot of business owners that are already established think, *oh, social media doesn't apply to my business*. It applies to every single business out there. You want to use platforms like LinkedIn, Facebook, Instagram, TikTok, use all of them. LinkedIn, especially business to business, to connect with professionals. A well-curated profile can make a very strong first impression on the internet.

In the digital landscape, regularly update your profile. If you have a profile from seven years ago, get it updated. Let's have it reflect relevant content that's applicable to what you're doing now. Engage with others' posts. Remember, we talked about the focus being others. If you shift your focus to other people and you show that what you're attempting to achieve is to provide others with value, focus on everyone else. You're going to come out ahead in every area of business. This rings true in leveraging social media. Comment on other people's posts, encourage them, empower them, lift them up through your responses, engage, create a connection, show that similarity of thought process, core beliefs, ethics, or methods, whatever it is. If you agree with it, let them know. If you agree with some of it, not all of it, acknowledge it, validate what they're saying, and then add to it. There's a way to add to it respectfully. That's going to be huge in networking and meeting people is leveraging those social media platforms. Another thing is preparing some conversation starters. Don't sound like a robot. You will not have this list of conversation openers and use the same two or three for each person. You're going to assess the situation and use what's best.

But you want to have some conversation starters in the back of your mind. When you approach someone or someone approaches you, you're not floundering, stuttering, figuring out what to say, coming across as unconfident or awkward. Have a list of some open-ended questions that are going to spark a two-way conversation. Have a set of topics that are ready. You can avoid awkward silences when there's a pause or a break in conversation. Obviously, you want to tailor those topics to what you're there to achieve, what everybody's there to learn. What's the topic of the conference, the summit, what are you there for? Let's create some topics around it, around yourself, and have some personal tidbits, passions, a hobby, something outside the realm of business. Because when you get to person 30 in the introduction process, you're going to be tired mentally and people are tired mentally. What do we do when we're tired mentally? We zone out, we tune it out. It's like hearing just another replica of what we just heard from the last person. We want to stand out. We want to be memorable, energetic, re-engage them, get them interested in networking at that event again. Give off that energy. One way is to connect with something outside of what you're there to accomplish that day, something personal, along with a relative topic.

In addition, you want to go into any networking event or networking opportunity, whether that's digitally, or it's in person, with the mindset of giving. The mindset of giving is about others. You want to approach networking with the mindset of what can you offer everybody else? What can you offer the people you meet? Not just what can I gain? Can I gain a customer, a sale, a vendor, or a better deal? Set that aside, go in with the objective of what can I give to everybody else? Think about how your skills, your knowledge, and your current connections within your network that you have already could benefit others. Sometimes it's just making an introduction to the right person. Make sure that you're attending diverse networking events. Don't limit yourself to industry specific events. Now, obviously, that does not mean that we go outside the realm and go to somewhere that has nothing to do with us. Don't say, you know what? I'm a dentist. I'm only going to dental specific events. No, open yourself up. Diverse networking can lead to unexpected and valuable connections. If I'm a dentist, I'm also going to some of the other medical practice networking events and I'm meeting other medical professionals, but not in the dental realm. That can open some synergistic opportunities. Open partnerships to refer, meet people in other industries where you can collaborate in what you're doing or partner together. You can explore different networking events, online webinars, online groups, Facebook groups, LinkedIn groups, and/or community gatherings. It doesn't have to be a networking event. It can be a community gathering. Sometimes I'll go to the Chamber of Commerce events. That's a great way to meet other business owners.

A community event that you're volunteering at. I will go intending to volunteer at a walk for the Immune Deficiency Foundation and I will meet other business owners that came and they're there for the same cause and we could connect over something that we have in common. They have a family member with an immune deficiency, and I can talk about my experience with my immune deficiency. It is important to go to different community gatherings and don't go intending to meet them to achieve something in your business. *Go to give back*. Sometimes I will use my restaurants to cater to different community events for free, especially when they're being hosted by other influential organizations that are doing so much for our community. I have inadvertently received many introductions where I've been able to make connections that were beneficial to me in business, but not for that purpose. It was an accident, but it was a fabulous side effect. Go to community gatherings, industry conferences, summits, and different trainings. Sometimes, there are local networking groups. You can go to breakfasts, lunches where there are various speakers, and not only do you make the great connections, but you learn something. You hear somebody else's experience and perspective, and it sparks an idea within your own mind, or it gives you valuable insights into another industry or a different way of doing something or a mistake that you can learn from.

Finally, remember that practice makes perfect. The more you network, the more you grow. Going to the doctor's office, the grocery store, shopping, a festival, or a restaurant. The more you practice introducing yourself to people, the more comfortable you become and the more effective you become at being able to identify your audience, who you're speaking to, and tailor a fantastic introduction that comes naturally. Challenge yourself to attend a certain number of networking events each month and to build your confidence and your comfort level of doing so. This doesn't have to be these expensive, $5,000 networking event. If you'd like to attend to that, that's great. But these can be free events, community events, festivals. It can be restaurants, a Chamber of Commerce event, summits, free webinars online, or free Facebook groups you join. Challenge yourself and write your goal of how many connections you'd like to make or how many events you'd like to attend, whether that's digitally or in person. Then at the end of the month, keep track. How many new people did I meet this month? See if it lines up with your goals and then readjust as necessary. Set those goals just like you set a goal for anything else in business. That's how you hold on to it and ensure that you stay on track with what you'd like to achieve. Remember that networking is not about being the most extroverted person in the room. You do not need to be an extrovert. Does it make it easier? Sure, but the more you practice, the more that becomes you. Remember, it's inside of each of us. We're not creating something new. We're dusting off something old that hides in there. Networking is about making a genuine connection. It's about meaningful interactions. Each opportunity to network is a chance to learn, grow, and expand your professional network. With practice and using these strategies that we're going to dive a little deeper into, you'll find that networking can become one of your most valuable tools for business success. It has been for me. A lot of clients will come to me and say, *OK, we need to spend on sales and marketing. What do we need to do operationally?* Those are important aspects of building, growing, or scaling a business. I think by far the most overlooked business growth tactic is those people dynamics, social smarts, people skills, and networking. People say, *oh, I don't have time for networking. I'm a business owner. I'm busy.* Make time. You can meet people in a lot of different situations without having to go to 100 events a month. Attempt to meet more people more often. Introduce yourself to more people more often. Don't shy away from it. Don't hide. You're going to see business growth if you network. It's an overlooked important key. Write down a goal of how many new people you want to connect with this month, whether it's personal or business, it doesn't matter. Write it down and then write down several networking events, groups to join, things you want to do to achieve that goal. Keep pushing through. Keep introducing yourself to more people more often.

In the next section, we will cover reading the room. When you go to an in-person networking event, or you're in a virtual networking event, the techniques are a little different, but the same foundation.

Reading the Room

In this section, we'll cover reading the room. Reading the room is essential when you attend a networking event in person. It allows you to quickly assess the social dynamics of the room, the mood, the energy level, and the feelings and emotions of those in attendance. Understand the overall environment so that you can navigate and engage with the people there effectively. The first thing you want to do is to not stay by the door. I want you to do a quick assessment. When I walk into a room, I immediately scan it. I take 10 to 20 seconds to scan it, then move away from the door. The best places to gravitate toward are a bar for drinks or a coffee bar. Gravitate there because 90% of people will stop for a drink or food. When I go into a room and look around, I first scan and look for the traffic patterns in and out. If people are mostly coming up on the left side, ordering here, and heading down to the right to pick up their drink, I want to go to the exit point. I migrate to that exit point because nobody wants to be interrupted when they first go up to grab their drink or food. Don't get to the front of the coffee table. No, no, no. Go to the end, where people are picking up their cocktails. Go to the end of the buffet. They have their plate of snacks, their tray of veggies, whatever it is, and now they're looking for where to go. That's where you meet a lot of people. I have gone to many conferences, and I can remember one specifically. I took a team with me, and we were on the panel, so we had already finished the panel discussion. There was a break for lunch, and we went and did that, and instead of going back into that training, I said, let's prepare for tonight's networking, and the team looked at me like I was crazy, "But Christy, everybody's going in there." I said, "Right, but we want to be strategic. We're going to do our networking at happy hour tonight." There was a little lounge that had hors d'oeuvres you could order. There was also a bar, a fantastic place to meet people. I made more connections during the two hours we spent at that lounge than during the three-day conference. Get yourself parked right there. Don't block the traffic, but get right over there. That way, when somebody's looking up and around, you can read that and say, great, they're looking for somebody to sit and talk to. Nobody wants to hold their drink, stand alone, hold a plate of food and snack alone, or sit alone. That's where you grab them and make your connection. That's the first tip. After you've taken a moment to observe the room, identify the traffic flow.

If there are no bars, coffee tables, buffet lines, or hors d'oeuvres areas, then the next thing you want to do is see the layout and what everybody is doing. Are they sitting at tables or standing together in groups? Force yourself to move away from the door. If there are no opportunities like that, the next thing you want to do is to look at everybody's body language. I scan different groups and immediately identify those with open body language. One thing to look for is that their feet are pointed outward and open with their shoulders and arms. That is typically an inviting pose. That is pointing themselves out to others, saying this circle is open for others to join. If you see a quiet conversation in the corner between two individuals, and their arms are crossed, or their closed backs are to the rest of the crowd, that means it's a little less inviting for somebody new to come up and join. You also want to identify, and you should know this before you get there. Is it a formal setting or casual? Is it people just mingling around the room? Are there assigned seats? Have people already established their seats in their little groups? It's vital to assess all that to determine how you want to move forward.

The next step is to identify those group dynamics. Pay attention to how people are grouped. Are they closed off? Is it an intimate circle that will be harder to weave your way into? Are they fluid groups? Are people moving from group to group? One of the successful ways to network at an Expo is to walk up and down, and many times, there are booths. You can go right up; people usually stand out there looking for people to join in a conversation and start talking. The great thing is once you engage, if you now display that open body language, that open positioning, point your feet out at someone, still be talking to who you're talking to, but also be open, slightly angled to the crowd that's coming in at the door or the crowd that's coming off the bar or the food area, and that is showing others that your group is open for newcomers. Be aware of that. Now, if you're in an intense one-on-one conversation and you'd like to wrap that up first, that's where you point your feet directly at the individual that you're looking and speaking to. There are different ways to do that. If you find a group standing in an open formation, they're more receptive to a newcomer joining, and that's where you want to start if there's no place to grab people outside the food and drink area. Listen to the tone as you approach, to the general buzz of that room. The venue, the volume, and the tone will clue you into what group you want to join. What's the mood here? Is this an agitated conversation? Is this an energetic conversation? Does this sound like people are in a good mood? Is somebody furrowing their brows and talking very low, and their body language is closed off to the rest of the room? You might not want to approach that group. A louder group with laughter can indicate a more casual atmosphere where people are comfortable. They're more receptive and in a positive mood. We want that.

I've gone into some quieter rooms, and it's a little more formal, a serious tone, very button up my jacket, business tone. You can mirror that, but there are still other subtle cues. You can look for nonverbal cues to see which group would be best to approach first. We want to look at the body language; are they relaxed, tense, engaged, disinterested, yawning, looking at their phone, looking at the ground, or looking at the door thinking, please, somebody else, come over here? You can read a bit of that to identify who will be most open and inviting for you to come up to. If you can find animated gestures, that will signify a positive and welcoming environment. I make it a point to create that environment in any group I join so we will attract the most people. It's like a magnet. How do you become magnetic and attract that attention? How do you draw people into your group to make the most of meeting new people? That's the goal. Introduce yourself to more people. We want to create that little net that pulls them in. We do that by focusing on how we're making everybody else feel. If we're giving off positive energy, smiles, our eyes are connecting with and smiling with others in the room, our posture is open and inviting, pointing a bit angled outward to show an invitation in, and we are relaxed, not stiff. It feels like that's where I want to go. We also look for that in others to determine where we want to start. That means facial expressions and eye contact. Is it a smiling face that's inviting you in? Is somebody making direct eye contact with you? Are they smiling with their eyes? Are they making eye contact and quickly looking down? Well, that means they might not be open to a connection, or they might be shy. Remember, this is not a 100% detector of these items, but these are the generalizations.

These are typical behaviors you're going to see in these situations. Note the energy level. Is this room or this group high energy? Is there a lot of movement, or is it more static? Have people settled into their spots at a table? Then, you want to adapt your approach accordingly. Match the group's energy level to blend in more naturally. I like to bring a little energy with me. However, if I see a group sitting quietly at a table, having a conversation, even if they are smiling or looking up and making eye contact, I will not rush over there and say, hi, I'm Christy Wilson. I will dial it back. Use that mirroring technique to come in, and if it's a more subdued group, it doesn't mean you can't be yourself. I will still bring that sparkle, energy, and passion, but I will do it in a more muted tone. I want other people to feel comfortable. My focus is on other people. Yes, this is me, but how can I make these people I'm approaching more comfortable? That's how I'm going to make the best connection.

Be mindful of varying comfort levels, including how direct you are, your personal space, and what's appropriate for that individual. You need to listen. Hear and read the person and the room and assess the most suitable situation. How can I make this individual feel comfortable? How can I connect with them? Be ready to adapt your approach. "Yes, I'm Christy, I'm high energy, I'm passionate, yes, I'm sparkly." I love to share that with others, but I base my approach on what I'm seeing around me, on my observations of the room and the groups within that room. In a more formal setting, I will have a more direct introduction. I'm going to be a bit more humorous in a casual setting. I'm just going to remain flexible. Be flexible, be ready to adjust your interaction style and approach, and note that if something's not working, it's okay.

You can move on to the next group. You can try it again and remain confident, because confidence is a choice. It's a set of behaviors. Remember that, and each time you go up to a group, you'll get a little better at reading that group. You're going to understand better how you want to portray yourself and what level of yourself you will display in that moment that's most appropriate for making the other person feel at their best and comfortable. Another thing is social cues. Look for social cues that show openness to a conversation. Individuals looking around the room or standing alone are shy and don't know how to integrate into a group. We can look at that approach for those individuals if it makes sense. If somebody looks like they don't want to be alone, yet are alone, and they're looking for interaction. Approach them. They're going to feel relieved. They're like, oh my gosh, I didn't have to do it. Somebody did it for me. Be the doer. Be the person who does that for others. Be the person who makes them feel comfortable. The other thing I do often is if I'm already in a group and may have a great conversation, but I see someone trapped at the door. I will often gesture to call them over. Sometimes, if I don't want to make a scene for them or I don't want to make them feel uncomfortable, I'll read that individual, smile at them, and make eye contact. A lot of times, they'll then approach. If you feel like somebody's standing alone and you exit the group at the right time, then gravitate over toward that person and include them into your next group or have them come with you or talk for a few minutes and say, "Hey, I wanted to go over there. I haven't introduced myself to that little group over there. Did you want to come along?" Take the lead and include them. That's a great way to form a connection. It gives you a buddy to go along with. Even though you're taking the lead, you will be that confident, the action doer, you will still have a wingman, you will have a person with you, and it will feel even more comfortable to approach those groups.

Finally, trust your gut. You do not have to be a pro at this. You will become a pro by practicing more often, but you'll never be perfect because, like I said, these are generalities. This is something to look for that works 99% of the time. But everything doesn't apply to every person and scenario. Trust your gut about when and how to engage with somebody based on what you're feeling and seeing. Tune into that person, set your focus, and ask, does this make sense? That can often guide you effectively in a social situation where you don't know who to approach or how to react. Follow that instinct if you feel drawn to a particular group or individual. It often leads to a significant interaction. One of the biggest things people tell me is that they are too afraid to do networking events or are not confident enough. Remember, confidence is a choice. I understand it's still scary, even though you're making that choice. I went to an event recently and felt like, who am I to be here? I don't belong here when I read up on the people in attendance. But then I remind myself, yes, you do. You had the invitation. Nobody's above anybody else. We shouldn't treat people like that, and we shouldn't feel that way around others. They're people. We all have that in common. They're multifaceted, complex people, just like ourselves. Just because they appear confident, that is a demonstrated set of behaviors. That's their choice. It's a habit, and it just comes out naturally now. But we don't want to let that fear hold us back. An excellent way to overcome that fear is to ask yourself, what is the worst that can happen? Well, I approached somebody, and they weren't very receptive. Move on.

You're going to find another connection. The more you do that, the more you'll be desensitized where it doesn't bother you. When I started many years ago in networking environments, I was a teenager working and attending these events. I felt out of place. I thought I didn't belong. I didn't feel good enough to be there. I had a lot of fear, but what if? What if this fails? I would approach someone, and if there wasn't that connection, I would feel defeated and like it was a failure. The more you do it, the more you will have people you don't connect with. You're not everybody's cup of tea, and that's okay. But how many fantastic connections and opportunities could you make if you opened the door within your business from going to these? Ask yourself, what's the worst that can happen? I didn't make a connection, so what? But what's the best that could happen? If you're saying, but what if they don't like me? But what if I can't connect with anyone? But what if? But what if you connect with people? Just one person and one connection can change your career or business trajectory. What if you miss out because of your what-ifs? That's always what I ask somebody. But you got something else out of it. If nothing else, more practice. You learned something from the event. You gained insightful experience.

You watched somebody else do something you saw you liked and resonated with you that you can use at a future event. I rarely find that it was a wasted hour. But what if you miss out? What if you don't do it? What is the risk there? Do a risk analysis. What if it all goes wrong? What if you don't make a connection? No harm, no foul. The risk level is low. But what if you miss opportunities because you are too fearful to attempt them? Start shifting your mindset away from what if you fail, what if you don't connect, and what if they don't like you. Shift them to what if you meet ten new people? What if I meet one new person who changes my career trajectory or business growth? What if I meet the right person who introduces me to somebody that changes my life? What if I meet some successful connections that I add to my network? What if I practice my skills to appear more confident, dusting off that confidence that lies inside me, and now I can do that more naturally in the future? What if I learn something great? What if I hear somebody's perspective that sparks an idea that I would have never had?

I feel like analyzing the risks because I'm a risk analysis gal. By assessing the what-if it goes wrong versus the what-if it went right, I think there's more risk in not going and attempting it in this case than if I go. I know this is hard to do. It's easier said than done. I always say you don't need someone else's validation. That does not mean you don't care about what somebody feels or thinks. That's the wrong thought process. Be aware of what others are feeling and thinking. You want to focus everything on others. That's how you succeed in business. However, you do not need someone's validation, and you do not need everyone to like you. You can be considerate of their feelings. You can do your best to deliver what they need in that moment to make them feel a certain way, but you do not need someone else's validation to move forward or appear a certain way. My kids say, "Easier said than done, Mom." But the more you do it, the more it becomes natural, and the more that becomes your mindset. Shift your perspective of what ifs with failing to what ifs with success. What if this happens? Get excited. What if I meet somebody who catapults my business forward? What if I meet a great connection, and we become fantastic friends, and we can learn from each other? What if I meet a successful mentor who gives me excellent business advice that prevents me from making detrimental mistakes within my business? What if the good, not what if the bad. Reading the room will blend observation, intuition, and adaptability. It will allow you to tailor your networking approach to fit into various social situations and environments. The more you practice and do it, the more natural it will be and the more comfortable you'll be in those situations.

You will learn from your last experience, apply that knowledge, and improve every time. Networking events are not a waste of your time; they are the growth of your business. They are the solution to scaling past seven or eight figures, so I encourage you to write, research some events in your area, and start out small. If you're uncomfortable, start out with a 10-person group or a five-person group, start out with something small, and then work your way up. You will be glad you did. Next, we will cover strategic conversational entry points. How can we strategically spark that conversation? That's going to be important when you're interacting and networking. Look up those networking events, write them down, and commit to them.

Strategic Conversational Entry Points

We are jumping back into mastering networking. We covered how vital networking is in your business. It just takes one introduction. It's all about who you know to change the trajectory of your entire business. I want you to not see networking as a chore or something you don't have time to do as a business owner. I want you to consider it one of the most important building blocks in growing your business and taking it past the seven and eight-figure mark. We'll focus on conversational strategic entry points in networking. Have you ever been in that position where you walk into an event and shift over to the edge of the room, scanning, and hiding in a corner, or you're camped out behind the coffee bar watching everybody else, and you feel awkward? An essential aspect of networking events is where you meet people and your strategic location. Have a strategy in place. When you enter the room, you want first to stop and scan the room and get a feel for who's there, what the environment's like, what the feeling is, what the attitude is, and what the energy level is. Scan the groups of people or individuals already there. Is it a group of invited individuals? Do they have an open body posture? Are they pointed out toward you? We will look at where we should stand this time. We covered how to be open to another individual. But I want to focus on where you stand because standing at the entryway is not a good place to be. Use that area to scan the room and determine your next move. I don't want you to pick a spot and hide in the corner somewhere, hiding behind the coffee bar. If there's a food or drink bar, one of the best places you can position yourself is not the beginning of that bar. No, no, no. Get your coffee. Get to the exit for that cocktail bar, food bar, coffee bar, whatever it is. Whatever is going on in that room, I want you to look at the traffic pattern of people coming up and exiting. I want you to position yourself strategically outside that exit. I do my best networking at cocktail hour. I have served on a panel many times, and it's been fantastic, and I've spoken at the conference.

But you don't get many networking opportunities when people are engaged in the conference, involved, or sitting at a table, and it's inappropriate to get up and move around. We want to take the opportunities and leverage the best position to make those connections. First thing, watch the traffic patterns when you see people going up to the cocktail bar, the coffee bar, or the food buffet, I want you to look at where they're coming in because when I come in, I'm walking in, and I'm focused on getting my drink and my plate. That's not where we want to intercept individuals. No, we want to be at the exit where the traffic exits that bar or that food buffet. Don't block the traffic coming out, but you want to position yourself right around there because what happens? You're walking down the bar; you have your coffee. You've finished your task. Your focus has been to get this coffee. You have your coffee cup, but what do you do? Now, people look around and often determine I want to go sit down. Their eyes come up. That's where you make your connection.

Make eye contact and smile; that's welcoming. Open body posture, your feet pointed toward them, the individual you want to meet. I know it sounds wild. They're a target, but it is like a bullseye. It's more about identifying or indicating to that individual that you are open to connecting. That's the perfect time when they look up and look for a second. Where do I go? They feel awkward and go into the corner. Instead, have that smile, open, inviting body language, and attitude about you. Make the first move. “Hey there, that looks good. I didn't see that in the bar.” Or, “How is the coffee?” I say something to break the ice. I know people dread small talk. I tell people not to do the typical small talk of opening up about the weather, but to find something relatable. Ask an open-ended question to engage in a more interactive conversation. It doesn't even have to be about the coffee. *What's been your favorite part of this conference so far?* Many people don't want to delve into work when taking a moment on a coffee break. *Which coffee did you get, the dark roast or the medium roast?* There are a lot of opportunities to connect to something more personal than the networking event. But strategically positioning yourself at that exit area for the food or drink bar will be an excellent place to connect with people and not be highly awkward because people will look to make that connection. That is a superb positioning location. The other place that works well is if there is no food or coffee bar, there's usually something. Still, if there isn't, if all else fails, and you haven't been able to connect with a group and you've entered and read the room, you don't know where to go from here; I want you to gravitate toward the center of the room or the center of the activity.

You're saying, oh no, I don't want to go to the center. I don't want to be front and center. I don't want to have the bullseye on my back, but you do because attending this event is to make meaningful connections. We want to go with the mindset of meeting new people and making authentic connections. We don't want to go with the mindset of I'm here to sell, get a client, get more business, and promote myself. It's about others and how you make them feel. That's why you focus on others when you position yourself at the end of the coffee or food bar. Is somebody else coming off that buffet or that bar, and they're feeling awkward and don't know where to go? You're here to make them feel fantastic. That's how you'll make your connection. When your focus shifts from you to others, it's all about making others feel a specific way. That's how you make good connections. It's a good mindset to have, too, because you'll be less focused on what you're doing. If you're feeling awkward and focused on somebody else and alleviating that for them, you will not dwell on it yourself.

If you think about an event you've been to, who's at the center? Well, the person who is comfortable, confident, and everybody's there to meet. When people walk to the door, they look around and see the center person. They're thinking, yeah, that's the person to be around. Remember, confidence is a choice. It's a set of demonstrated behaviors. It is a skill. Strategically position yourself in the center of the activity or at the exit of those locations. When you get there, keep that eye contact. Make eye contact with people. You don't have to hold it. It's tough for me, but I still do it. If I have to look down and then at somebody else or shift my gaze, that's okay. But make sure that you're making eye contact. Make sure you have that energy flowing out of you that you hyped yourself up about before walking into that room and positioning yourself. Make sure you radiate that positivity because the first rule when strategically positioning yourself is to have a smile, not just in your mouth and face, but also in your eyes. Connect that eye contact, and your eyes need to smile. That's an inviting feature. It's welcoming them to come over and engage in conversation. You are pointing your feet toward the group of people coming or the individual coming. Ensure you're giving off that positive feeling and energy. Nobody wants to be around negativity. Negativity attracts attention. That's when we talk about hooks in marketing and getting people's attention. Why? Well, we're wired that way. We are wired to heed warnings. When we hear something negative, it grabs our attention because we are wired to listen, so we don't make that mistake. But positivity holds attention, keeps people. Negativity attracts attention initially, but positivity will keep it. That's what will draw people to a networking event. Nobody wants to be around someone with a sour attitude or look. We are drawn to positivity. We are drawn to smiles and inviting behaviors. If you want to attract people to yourself, then you need to get out there, either in the center or in a strategic location. If there's something else going on, there's a line, or there's a signing of a book. I will sometimes position myself at a large conference table outside the exit, where people check in and pick up their badges. Because if there's no coffee bar or place like that, that's an excellent area because they have their swag bag, lanyard, and they're looking at a schedule, and they're thinking, oh shoot, what do I do now? That's an excellent place to connect and engage.

That's another option. You need to place yourself strategically somewhere. I have been to many speaking events, conferences, and summits, speaking there and taking part in them. Some of my most successful networking happens over cocktail hour when people are more relaxed. Do not skip out on the morning breakfast or the cocktail hour. Do not skip out on those after-hours pieces. Don't say, well, I checked the box; I went to the conference. You can make the best connections when someone has exited that environment, and that work mindset, and their guard is down. They are automatically in that mode that is more welcoming and easier to connect with, to talk with them about things outside of work, which will make a stronger connection and bond. I have had times when I've spoken or participated in a panel, left for some of the other training that did not pertain to me, and parked myself down at the little table right outside the traffic pattern exits of the bar. At cocktail hour at 5:30, when people started coming in to grab a drink or a bite to eat, that is where I've seen more success than anything else during that event. Remember that strategically placing yourself somewhere in the center of where people are going is not at the beginning, but at the end. When they've looked up and said, oh, now what? That's where you make your connection. This is going to require recognizing and utilizing these entry points to build rapport at the right time and gather information about the other person. Remember, your focus is on that other person, how you make them feel, and your active listening. What is active listening? It is not listening to respond. It's listening to understand. You are looking to empathize. You are looking to put yourself in their shoes.

Get a full picture of how that individual is feeling, thinking, and conveying. Understand that you can make a good connection and build rapport. This also allows you to share knowledge and position yourself as an authority in a specific space. It can also position you as somebody that people want to be around. People want to be around positive energy. They don't want to be around someone slumped over in the corner, with a sour look on their face, looking stressed out at their phone, scrolling through, furiously typing an email. Put that aside when you're in networking mode. Go to the restroom if you need to beforehand in front of the mirror. I am so-and-so, and I do XYZ best. I am so excited. I'm here to meet people. Hype yourself up. Get excited about meeting all these people and all these opportunities. To create that valuable connection, we need to ensure we're at the right strategic location and looking for cues to enter the conversation appropriately. That means you have to start the conversation, but we want the other person talking more than you, because that's how you're going to learn. That's how you will respond effectively and make that relatable connection. People are drawn to similar things. That relatability, they want that commonality. Give that to them. Listen to what they're saying. Pick up on those little cues and weave them into the conversation. Look for the shared interests. Listen for mentions of challenges or needs you can address or even share insights on handling them. Even if it's not from a sales perspective because, remember, this is just that initial connection. Being able to offer suggestions about things that have worked, or resources, can be very helpful to someone. That builds a connection, and people often feel a sense of reciprocity. I want to give something back to you now. That's not why we do it, but it is a natural behavior or a natural side effect of offering something valuable.

I had an instance at my last networking event in Atlanta. I saw that someone was going down the wrong hallway. I had already been down there, and I knew that there was nothing down there. I stopped them and helped. We talked on the way back. Even though we were splitting off into different conference rooms, we exchanged business cards and had a moment of connection. I learned about this individual three or four minutes after our connection to just a simple help offer. Active listening is essential for identifying a good entry point in a conversation. Don't just hear the words; understand the context and emotions behind them; listen to what they're saying and then watch for what they're not saying. Practice by focusing entirely on the other individual, noting their body language, tone, underlying message, and everything about them. Then, use empathy to understand and relate to their feelings. Even if you have not experienced that exact thing. You can relate somehow and make that connection.

Speak clearly and concisely at networking events. Articulate things clearly. You don't want to be confusing. You don't want to be jumping all over. Sometimes, here, we bounce topic to topic as it comes up. But when I'm at a networking event, I stay focused on what they're talking about and stick to a specific message I'm conveying. That's crucial. Practice tailoring your language and your tone to your audience. You can use some mirroring if you'd like to at that point. We don't want to go overboard. Remember, with mirroring, people like to feel similar. That can be an essential connection builder. Use those open-ended questions to encourage a discussion, not just small talk about the weather. Open-ended conversations, things that are engaging, will reveal more opportunities for that strategic engagement.

Research the attendees and the topics of the networking event before going. Be knowledgeable. You don't want to get there and not know what's going on, who's speaking, or what sessions are happening. That does not allow you to offer that helpfulness. It does not allow you to engage in a knowledgeable conversation with someone. You also want to understand who you will meet with and who will be there because there is no cocktail event at this thing. It's a breakfast or a brunch situation. It's going to be coffee or a breakfast buffet. Understand what it is you're walking into. Do your research first, whether you're talking to a client, networking event, or team member. You want to be prepared so that you know your audience and can prepare some conversation starters ahead of time or some questions related to your field or common interests. But don't rely solely on them. Sometimes, wing it. You will get better at that. Practice it daily with people you meet at the grocery store and family members. Practice just segwaying into a conversation that you didn't prepare for. That's a good way to get better at it. It will become more natural. Observe body language and social cues. If somebody's firing away keys on their laptop or phone, they're busy and not really a great person to approach. If somebody is pretty closed off, you want to read whether they're shy and feeling awkward or closed off and not open.

Read the people, constantly assessing, analyzing, and adjusting—adapting as you see who you're talking to. Your core values don't change. I'm still Christy. My core values are the same. My personality is the same. However, to make the other individual comfortable and open to a connection, it's all about making them feel a specific way. Mirroring makes people feel comfortable. It does not mean you have to be fake, but you can adapt your approach to ensure that you give that individual what they need to make a meaningful connection. It's just like with your team members. You're not being fake because you use one approach with this individual and one approach with that individual. You're adapting your strategy to make it meaningful and comfortable for others. Your focus should be on everyone else around you and how you make them feel.

Remember, that's all charisma is. It makes people feel a certain way with a demonstrated set of behaviors. Confidence is just a skill. You want people to feel comfortable and show genuine interest in others' perspectives, whether you agree or not. You do not have to agree with everything, but you can be interested in what someone else says. You can use entry points to provide valuable insights, assistance, and connections to the other person, letting them know you met someone over there who does X, Y, and Z when you hear them discussing that. Position yourself as a resource for everyone there, a problem solver, and a positive energy at that event, and that will benefit everyone else. If your focus is on others, you will do better at the networking event. Mirroring matching allows you to suddenly mirror body language or speech patterns to make people feel more comfortable. Don't overdo it. That seems weird and insincere. Use open-ended questions. Encourage others to talk more about themselves and their interests. You'll learn more, and it will be better for you. Opportunity-wise, it reveals more potential entry points for that strategic conversation. Use stories, analogies, and memorable things to grab attention and make points more engaging. Relate your experiences or relevant anecdotes to that conversation in a story form. Open with a story and you will be more memorable. A better connection, and then your responses should show that you understand and care about the other person's point of view and what they're saying. Respond in a way that acknowledges their feelings. When you find an entry point, contribute valuable insights, and help when appropriate. Don't just talk to talk. Let others speak more. That's how you learn, and that's how you can be more strategic. Share relevant knowledge, connections, and resources that are helpful. Remember, you aim to be a problem solver and a valuable resource.

That's why you see those people in the middle of the room, and you're thinking, oh, wish I could be that. Look, they're the life of the party. It's like a magnet. Everyone's drawn to them. It's their energy, positivity, behaviors, and their mannerisms. Most of all, it's how they make others feel around them. It's about being valuable and a helpful resource to others. Practice it. Reflect on what worked and what didn't. If you made a mistake, it was no big deal. That's part of you. It's fine. It's more authentic, but you can identify some missed opportunities or successful entry points that you could have done and don't dwell on them or beat yourself up, but use it as a learning experience to prepare for the next time. Seek feedback. You can go to mentors afterward and talk about a specific situation. Gain some feedback on your interactions and conversational skills. Then, keep up to date with industry trends and news so that you have something to fall back on to talk about that will grab people's attention at these events. Continuous learning will enhance your ability to be more conversational and create meaningful connections. Practice it in everyday conversations and attend networking events to refine your skills further.

You will not read this and think I'm a pro. It takes practice. It requires developing a keen sense of observation. It requires practicing your empathy skills. It requires practicing effective communication skills. Make sure that you are using variation in your voice. Nobody wants to hear a robotic script. They have tuned you out. Our brains are wired to do so. Have inflection, vary the volume, practice coming in faster on something you want to get out quickly, and then slow it down to emphasize a specific point. There are different things you can do to regain that attention. Practice those communication skills, and by preparing and practicing daily, reflecting on daily interactions, networking interactions, you will enhance your ability to navigate and leverage conversations strategically.

The goal is to create mutually beneficial relationships and position yourself as a valuable connection in your professional network. That's how you'll gain authority and become that go-to resource. Strategically placing yourself at the right location at a networking event. I don't want you to memorize those scripts. I want you to use them as a guide or as a fallback. If you panic and don't know where to go, you can use one of those open-ended questions to re-engage the conversation. Have a couple in your back pocket. Hype yourself up before walking into that event, and step outside your comfort zone. Don't hide in the corner or at the back of the bar. Focus on gravitating toward the center, becoming the point at which other people are now gravitating around. Look for opportunities like the end of that coffee bar or the end of that food buffet. Position yourself in a place that makes sense after watching the traffic patterns of the room and determine where is best to grab somebody where they're not starting a task; they're finishing, and now they're going to be looking up for somewhere to go. How can we make other people there feel less awkward? How can we make them feel more welcome and invited? If you take nothing away from this entire chapter, I want you to take away that networking is about others. Like everything else in your business, it's about focusing on others. How can you make them feel? How can you be a valuable and helpful resource? How can you be that connection that people want to make? How can you help other people be that strategic problem solver, the person giving the go-to resources, the go-to advice, and insights that are relevant and helpful? If you master that, you've mastered networking. I want you guys to be pros. Be confident to attend a virtual event or an on-site networking conference, summit, or event. Implement a bit at a time. Remember, small steps are okay. Behaviors turn into habits. Habits are then how people view us. If you want to own the room, if you're going to give off that likable feeling, that charismatic personality, if you want to be the go-to, the magnet at these events, practice.

Owning the Room-Commanding Presence

We've talked about how important networking is. Networking is an essential part of your business growth. If you want to grow as a business and surpass seven figures this year, you must focus on networking for many reasons. Number one, it allows you to seek new opportunities. Business is all about who you know. Number two is successful connections and resources for vendors, mentors, and other people in the industry and learning about your competitors. Networking can also lead to better sourcing for your team members as you grow and need your team to succeed. Networking is a positive thing for businesses. Don't look at it as a chore, a task you don't have time for. People are your business. Therefore, networking is connecting yourself to more people. You're building your network and, thus, building your business.

Let's talk about owning the room. When you see or think of that person who owns the room at an event, they command everyone's attention. People are drawn to them. They're exciting. They give off this incredible energy. They're just comfortable with who they are and what they're saying. They are experts. Because of that confidence, you think they're the go-to. They are the person to talk to at this event. If you practice, it will be you. Let's start with some key points we want to practice daily. It will not happen overnight, so you'll start small. You're going to practice implementing these tips in your everyday life. It will improve your ability to network, whether at an event, meeting somebody randomly at the post office, the grocery store, the mall, or wherever you are. It will help you build your confidence in networking, meeting new people, and building stronger connections. The first thing we will discuss is confident body language. Your body language speaks volumes before you even say a word, so let's stand or sit tall. Maintain good posture. Keep your shoulders back and use open gestures when talking or networking. You don't want closed gestures because they make you seem closed off and unapproachable. Be open. Take up the surrounding space. We don't want to intrude into other people's space, but we want to take up our space. It's comfortable. It's going to make you feel more confident and comfortable. It's proven. It works.

Practice your power poses before you enter a room. Go to the restroom. Do it before you leave. Do it in your rear-view mirror in the car. If you're coming in an Uber, like I said, there are public restrooms. You can do it at a hotel. That will help you boost your confidence before you even get to that door so that you can read the room and strategically place yourself, as discussed earlier. Poses that make your body expansive and open are power poses. Pause on power poses momentarily and ensure you understand what that means. My go to is hands on my hip. But it doesn't have to be. It can be one hand on a hip and one down. Open palms. Expansive. Take up your space. That is associated with increased feelings of confidence and assertiveness. Not aggressiveness, but assertiveness. Other people will view it as more confident and assertive. You will feel more confident and assertive. Stand with your hands on your hips, but you want your feet spread apart a bit. Don't crunch up. I know it's a habit sometimes to crunch in and feel a little smaller to take up less space when you're feeling less confident, but that's the opposite of what we need to feel confident. Feet apart. Eyes out. Even if you have trouble making eye contact like I do with people, you want to shift your gaze around. Be smiling with your eyes, with your mouth when it's appropriate. Be nodding, giving off that positive vibe and energy. People will pick up on it. People like and are drawn to positivity. Positivity holds your attention and reels people in. They want to be around somebody confident, not arrogant. You must be confident in your abilities, what you're saying, and your desire to be open to meeting people, hearing their perspectives, and learning about them. When you walk in there, walk in with your shoulders back. When you're standing, power poses. Feet apart. Take up your space.

Sometimes, it's a virtual event. You sit at tables when people are speaking or talking, or it's a lunch-and-learn and an open discussion. You can stretch your arms out if it's appropriate. What you don't want to do is fold up your hands and cross everything off. I know we were taught to cross our legs. Keep everything uncrossed, open, and pointed out. The science behind power poses. Let's touch on that for just a second. Studies show that adopting these poses can increase the confidence hormone or testosterone. It can decrease your cortisol level, which is your stress hormone. It decreases those levels in the brain while increasing your confidence hormone. You appear more confident to others and feel more confident because the chemicals are balancing the opposite way. Your confidence hormone is going up. You've got stress hormones going down. That's going to make you feel less stressed and more confident inside. That's going to make it easier to convey that confidence to others. Practice before the meeting, before the event, and before meeting with a client or a new employee; it doesn't matter who it is. Spend a few minutes in a power pose before the business engagement. Do it in a mirror if you need to. Find private space. Pose for about two minutes. It's going to help boost your confidence. It sounds silly. Do it in the privacy of your home or before you leave your car. I don't care where you are, but do it. It works. Integrate your power poses into your daily routine. It builds a habit of confidence. Remember, behaviors convey confidence. When we practice those behaviors, what do they become? Habits. Then habits are what you're viewed as. "Yeah. Christy's confident." It's just a habit. It's my go-to because I practice it often. Integrate it into your daily routine.

Let's talk now about eye contact. I know this is tough for many. It is tough for me. However, eye contact is the key to establishing a connection initially. It conveys confidence. It conveys attentiveness. Be smiling with your eyes. It draws people in. It's that open, welcoming feel you're giving off. Make eye contact with various individuals in the room, not just the ones you're speaking to directly, to indicate that you're open for others to join you when you're making eye contact, even if you can't hold that eye contact. I understand you can't always hold it. Use it to look up when you're talking. Use it to look at the next person. Just make the connection and then shift to the next. But the more you practice it, the more it will become a habit and the easier it will become. Think about it when you're practicing, but don't think about it there. Just think of it as you're focused on that person. It's natural to look up and make that connection with your eyes.

Next, there is controlled vocal delivery. A steady, clear, and confident voice commands attention in a room. Besides that, I found that having that smile in your voice, having that energy that radiates out of your voice, will also draw people's attention. People are drawn to positivity. They like to feel good. They want to be around good energy. Even if you're not feeling very energetic, what happens when you walk up, and you feel you're in a slump, and you're talking with someone that has that energy and is conveying that smile in their voice and is drawing you in with what they're saying? It's contagious. It's hard not to boost your mood a bit. That's why people are drawn to that. Practice it daily. It will draw people to you. Practice speaking at a moderate pace. Use pauses to emphasize points effectively. Use vocal variety, meaning sometimes you're going to speed up faster, and it's going to re-engage someone's brain. When you shift or change the way you deliver your words, your vocal variety, and what you're projecting vocally, when you change, it re-engages the other individual's brain and grabs attention. You don't want to sound monotone the entire time. Sound excited. You don't have to sound over the top. You don't have to be a cheerleader. But you want to have energy and vocal variety. Slow down on the points you want to emphasize. Use your body language to help you. I use my hands when I'm emphasizing a point. It's like everything's slower. But then sometimes it's exciting. You're going a little faster. Your body language, words, and vocal variety should adjust based on what you're saying. That will come naturally as you practice it more. It will become a habit because it's a practiced skill. It becomes who you are. The more we practice a skill, the more it becomes a habit. The more it becomes our go-to behavior, the more people view that as who we are. Practice that daily. Practice the vocal variety and raise the voice on something exciting. You don't have to shout at somebody. But raise that volume level. Then take it down when you're emphasizing something. Use that vocal variety to re-engage their brain continuously. It makes it more interesting, makes you more memorable, and makes people not want to fall asleep. Use storytelling, engaging stories, analogies, or things that people remember. They will be drawn into your conversation more.

The next thing is to dress for success. What does that mean? First, your attire. I do not care what anybody says. I had someone at one of my restaurants mention to me. "Christy, how you dress, and your appearance are not really judged the same way they used to be." Just because things are acceptable today does not mean that your appearance does not influence how you're perceived. That's still a thing. You can't change that first impression that people get. It's wired into us. Dressing appropriately for an occasion can enhance your presence. That does not mean you must dress stuffy in something you are not confident in. Choose attire that matches the occasion, which is professional but also makes you feel confident and comfortable. What that means is—for example, me. I wear heels all the time. I can count the times that I wear flat shoes in a year on one hand. I'll put on my slides when running on the treadmill or on the beach. I'm comfortable in heels. When you're wearing something you're not confident in, it makes it difficult to display those confident behaviors. I like things that reflect my personality. I like sparkle; aside from the heels, sparkle makes me feel like me. When I go up on stage, I'll sometimes wear a sparkly blouse underneath a professional blazer, if it's appropriate. When I was speaking in Vegas recently at a leadership conference, it was totally appropriate. When I went to a conference that was a bit more business dressed, I knew everybody was going to be coming in suits and ties. I wore a suit with a fresh white button-down I liked, which had a fun pattern woven into the white. I wore a navy suit with it and closed-toed conservative heels. You can still stand out with something comfortable and confident, whether a piece of jewelry, a pair of shoes, a cufflink, a tie, a shirt, a blouse, a skirt, or a particular style. Whatever makes you feel like you and makes you feel confident. Make sure it fits the occasion. Regardless of what anybody tells you today, your attire can influence how you're perceived. Keep that in mind. People are naturally drawn to stories. Use that storytelling to your advantage. It helps make your communication more engaging and memorable. Incorporate relevant personal anecdotes. Business stories that illustrate your points effectively.

I was speaking on a podcast just a couple of weeks ago, discussing the answer to a question: Do *you believe we should use data-driven decisions or decide based on more experience and intuition?* My answer was a holistic view. It should be 85% data-driven and about 15% intuition. Intuition is typically just your subconscious pushing back or pushing up your experience and memories. Your intuition comes from a specific experience or somebody else's experience that you learned from. It's that holistic approach. Pick something that's going to stick out, to make yourself and your message more memorable. You want something that sticks out, is easy to listen to, memorable, and easy to digest so that the audience can take away important key points from that message and remember them by associating them with something, whether a visual, an analogy, or a story. Storytelling helps to engage the audience and make your message and yourself more memorable.

Next is authenticity. Authenticity resonates with people. Be genuine in your interactions. I know we've talked a lot about different behaviors that we display, such as mirroring others, confidence, and charisma. That's good. Those are habits and behaviors. But authenticity, who you are, that doesn't change. That's one of those core values we discussed—your why, mission, and core values don't change. Your personality doesn't change. I can tone down Bouncy Christy and Cheerleader Christy, but I will not make Cheerleader Christy go away. That's okay, because you will not be everybody's cup of tea. You should stay true to who you are. Even though you're showing, displaying specific behaviors, you're still you. Your core values don't change, and neither does who you are. How you convey that message doesn't change. Share your genuine thoughts and experiences in a way that applies to the audience and the context. Authenticity is always a winner. If you're feeling unconfident, go to the bathroom, get your power pose going, and then look and say, I am (whoever you are); I am me, and I can't mess that up. I do it better than anyone else. While you're doing it, keep your power pose going. Remember that we care about what people think. We care about others, but we don't require validation from others. Your core values, who you are, doesn't change. You don't need validation from others to be your authentic self and display your core values and personality. Self-confidence or authentic confidence starts with self-awareness. That's understanding your strengths, areas for growth, and opportunities. It comes from a realistic appraisal of your abilities. Reflect on your accomplishments and challenges regularly.

However, self-awareness is the first step in building authentic confidence. Positive self-talk. Don't interact negative thoughts with positive affirmations. That does not mean that we don't look at a mistake we made or an opportunity, reflect on it, but don't dwell on it. We do a lot of good. One bad does not cancel out all the good you've done. Counteract those negative thoughts and leave the requirement for validation from others at the door. Focus on others and the value you can provide to them, the help you can give them, what you can do for them, what you can offer them, the solutions you can provide, and the feeling you can give them, lifting them up, empowering them, making them feel good, giving them warm fuzzies. Replace your thoughts like, *I can't do this* before you walk into a room with, *I'm prepared to do this, and I am competent. I am (your name), and I do it better than everybody here.* Try that before you go into a situation where you feel less confident.

Competence leads to confidence. Remember, practice leads to confident behaviors. Competence leads to confidence. Develop skills and expertise in your field. As your competence grows, your confidence in those skills will also increase. Invest in continuous learning and professional development. Learn from others' perspectives. Always be open and looking to learn new things daily. That will help you build on that authentic confidence. Be genuine in your interactions. Authenticity fosters genuine confidence and connection. Remember, opening with a compliment is excellent, but only if it's authentic. Don't tell somebody something to flatter them. Find something that resonates with you, or you didn't notice, and authentically uplift that individual. Focus on being present and engaging sincerely during your conversations.

Finally, mindfulness and stress management: Manage stress and stay present. Release that self-doubt, that nervous behavior. Remind yourself, power pose. I am. You do it better than anyone else. I don't require validation. I'm competent in this. I'm here to meet people. I'm excited about this and the opportunity I'm presented with, and I'm dropping the stress because high stress can undermine my confidence. Practice relaxation techniques regularly. If you're about to speak, prep beforehand. I'll turn up the music in the car and sing along. I will think about something that gets me excited about something coming up. I will think about something I did well this past week and engage if I can. When I take that focus off myself, and I put it onto someone else, it helps relieve some of that stress and anxiety. Really focus on authentic confidence building and being yourself, holding true to your core values and your why. This will empower you to navigate business environments more effectively and create stronger professional relationships. Remember, confidence is not about portraying perfection but about embracing your abilities and presenting them confidently, presenting yourself, and demonstrating behaviors that show that confidence. It's not about perfection. Some of the most charismatic people are vulnerable in showing their imperfections. Those imperfections are what we love about them the most. It's not about perfection, but about embracing your abilities into positive energy. Bring a positive and enthusiastic energy into the room with you. Positivity is contagious.

Even when we're in a bad mood, we are drawn to positive things. It's contagious, and it sets the tone for the interaction. Have a positive mindset going into it. Before entering the room, have yourself in a positive mindset. Practice your power pose, hype yourself up, and maintain it throughout your interactions. If you bring positivity, you will be a magnet, attract everyone to you, and own the room. You are going to display confidence and provide value to individuals. Make sure you show genuine interest in others. Listen actively, not to respond, but to understand. That way, you can respond thoughtfully and with a focus on the other person. Ask questions and provide responses, showing that you've fully engaged in the conversation. Remember to put yourself in their shoes. See things through their lens. That's going to help you make those authentic connections. You must position yourself in the room carefully because it will affect your ability to command presence.

If possible, position yourself where you can be easily seen and heard by everyone or most of the group. The head of the table, the center of the table, or the center of the room. We discussed positioning yourself at the end of a coffee bar, food buffet, or cocktail bar. Get yourself to a good place with a lot of traffic, which draws people to that energy you'll give off. That allows people to come up to you because you're open, warm, inviting, and have an open body posing and positioning. Your feet are pointed out to groups. You have confidence. You're smiling with your mouth and eyes. You are genuinely welcoming, and people are drawn to you. They're like, that's where I want to be. That's the person I want to meet. Make people want to be around you and meet you. It's all about how you make someone else feel.

How you make someone else feel is charisma. Owning a room is the same thing. The same rules apply. Use up your space. Don't make yourself small. Don't be looking down. Resist the temptation to pull out a phone and scroll through it. You might feel awkward; let me do something. But you're now giving off this feeling of being unapproachable. Use up the surrounding space effectively. Move around if it's appropriate. It can keep the audience's attention if you're speaking or talking to someone, especially if you're presenting. Use hand gestures. Move around the stage. Engage different sections of the audience. Make sure you speak to everyone and treat everyone like they are a VIP because they are. They are all significant individuals. They are all individual people. Make each of them feel special because, remember, being memorable, delivering a message that's memorable, and making a memorable connection is all about how you made the other person feel and what you could offer them. What problem-solving value can you offer to others? Owning a room is about combining confidence, authenticity, and engagement. Those three make up the perfect recipe for owning the room. It's about presenting yourself, interacting with others, how you make them feel, and conveying your words and message. Remember, a commanding presence is never about dominating the conversation. Speak less than the other people around you. It's about creating a space where your confidence and authenticity encourage others to engage and want to connect with you. With practice, these strategies are going to help you develop a presence that's commanding and approachable. You're going to be a memorable figure in any professional setting. If you practice this now, it will become second nature. You will get better at it every time and be able to own the room, those networking events, relationships, and new connections.

Next, we're going to touch on exit strategies. I know that exiting a conversation can be difficult. We talked about strategic entrances to the conversation, owning the room, and different networking strategies. But one thing that gets left off a lot is how to exit a conversation gracefully, in a classy manner, in a way that still makes that individual feel that they are a VIP and that you are not abruptly leaving the conversation.

Networking Exit Strategies

We've covered networking for business success and how to become a networking master. We've gone over a lot of strategies. Hopefully, you found them helpful; I have not put you to sleep yet, and this resonates with you. These are tips and tricks that you can use and start practicing in your everyday life to become a networking master. This is second to business growth and strategy. I want to cover keys to exiting a conversation. Because so many times you go to a training about how to connect with others, how to open up conversations, what are some icebreakers. If you panic, if you are out of conversation starters, that's where you're going to want to use an appropriate one from the list. But one thing that people miss out on in those trainings is how to exit a conversation. It is important because you've done all this work to connect with this person and build a relationship. Then at the end, you're just like, "Okay, we'll talk, bye." I mean, I'd be thinking I was abrupt. Or

“Okay, I'm going to leave now.” Or you just walk away. I've had people just walk away. Let's talk a bit about how to exit a conversation in a classy, non-awkward, and calm manner that still allows you to make that individual feel or that group feel they are important. They are heard; they mean something to you, and you're not just cutting off a conversation. Tact is required. Let's tactfully exit a conversation, but sometimes we want to make it to another contact. I'm all about quality over quantity, but we also want to meet a good amount of people because the more people we meet, the more opportunities that creates. You need to build your network faster. Let's talk about how to make both parties feel respected, so the interaction ends on a positive note.

One way to do it is to offer a genuine compliment or gratitude. People appreciate recognition and positivity. The important thing is to make sure that it's authentic because they can smell fakeness a mile away. Plus, we don't want to give off that vibe. We don't want to say something just to appease or just to get something out of somebody. We want to genuinely empower and uplift others. If you do that and you make that your mindset and your business, your business will grow. People appreciate genuine recognition and positivity. They're drawn to it. Compliment something specific that you enjoyed about the conversation or thank them for their insights. Something like, *I really appreciate your insights on X, Y, Z. It's really given me a lot to think about, a great takeaway for me. Thanks so much.* Then you can exit out gracefully. Or, *you know what? I really love what you said up there about X, Y, Z. It has given me so much to go home and research or really a starting point for me to implement this in my business. Thank you so much.* Then you can gracefully exit the conversation. It doesn't leave it open-ended, doesn't make anybody feel awkward. That’s something to keep in mind. The next thing is going to be future-oriented. What does that mean? Mention a future point of contact to follow up with, so it suggests continuity. It leaves the door open for future interactions with this person. Something like, *I'd love to continue this discussion. Can I email you next week?* Or *I'd love to continue this discussion. Are you good with us connecting on LinkedIn so that we can continue to discuss X, Y, Z?* Or, *I love all of your insights, and I'd love to continue our connection over X, Y, Z. Are you open to me calling you next week, Tuesday afternoon?* Something that allows you to wrap up the conversation, but also tells them I'm so interested that I want to continue this. Just because I want to move on in networking right now, I felt we made a connection, and I would love to continue this in a future interaction. That is something you can use to exit out gracefully.

Another tip to gracefully exiting a conversation is to introduce them to someone else. Be helpful. Introduce them to someone that is going to allow them to make another connection too. We want to help others. Facilitating connections for others is a valuable trait. You did something for them too. Made them feel good about it and helped them out. If possible, when doing this, introduce them to someone else at the event that helps to create a new conversation for them that makes sense within their industry. An example might be, *have you met Christy over here? You two might have a lot in common. You're both in the digital marketing world.* Or *you and John over here would really hit it off because you are both into golf. I was talking to so-and-so earlier, and she mentioned she was looking for someone who is knowledgeable around insurance. Now, hearing you say this, would you mind if I introduced you to her?* Something like that. Then you're able to take them over, make a warm introduction, and exit out to move on to your next opportunity.

Another thing that you can use is excusing yourself for a reason. Providing a reason for leaving is going to be more socially acceptable and less abrupt than just walking away. You can excuse yourself for a networking related reason, like meeting someone or attending a session. *Oh, this has been so great. I really appreciate these insights you've shared. I need to catch up with a colleague before they leave, but it was great talking to you.* You can also say, *oh gosh, I noticed that the next session is starting, and I want to make sure that I get in there. I'm so excited to see so-and-so. Are you going to be joining the session as well?* But that's a little less abrupt than just saying goodbye and leaving. You can also close with a non-committal but polite remark. It signals the end of the conversation without the awkwardness. You can make a general polite remark about enjoying the event or the session you were just in. For example, *oh, I'm going to mingle a bit more, but it's been good chatting with you. I'm glad we met today.* That's a little less awkward than just, okay, I'm going to go. You can just be honest. *I'm going to refill my coffee because two o'clock hits and I felt that energy zap. It's been so good talking with you. If it's okay, let me give you my business card and I would love to connect over coffee.* Or *I'd love to call you and talk shop a little more.* It's even better if you can connect and relate to something personal. *I wanted to pass you the name of the dog groomer I use. I was so happy because of having a dog with similar needs, is it okay if we exchange cards and I email you next week? When I get back into the office, I'll shoot you that groomer's information.*

Another thing is offering a handshake or gesture. Physical gestures like a handshake can sometimes signify the end of an interaction. Extend your hand for the handshake or another appropriate gesture as a sign of closure. While reaching out, you can say, *it's been such a pleasure meeting you. I'm so glad that we ran into each other and could connect. Before I move over there to catch up with John, let me give you my business card. I'd love to connect next week and get a time on the calendar to talk a bit more about XYZ.* Or *I'd love it if we could add each other as contacts and stay in touch. We both love baseball so much. We love the same team. Yay Braves,* whatever it is. Something can be added in rather than just the handshake. I would avoid doing just the handshake, but you can add the handshake in to signify the end of that conversation and then use another one of your exit strategy statements. Personalize these, make them yours. Don't take mine verbatim, put them into your words, your personality, make it you. You can connect to the event. Redirecting the focus to the event feels natural and less personal, like you're leaving for personal reasons. Reference a part of the event that you're moving onto next. *I'm going to head over to the next talk now, but enjoy the rest of the event and stay in touch. Shoot me an email. I'm so excited to hear how your daughter's XYZ season went. I know you drove six hours to get here, so make sure you drive safely.* Something a little more personal. Show interest in their participation. Ask them about their plans for the rest of the event as you close out. *Oh, you know what? I'm going to head over to that next talk now. Which session are you planning to attend next?* You can start with *which session are you planning to attend next? I see that they're starting in about five minutes. I know we're going to want to get a great seat. Are we going to the same one or different ones? I'd love to hear your thoughts on what you get to see in XYZ. You know, we can catch up over coffee next week and discuss what we learned.*

Remember, the goal is to exit the conversation in a way that maintains that connection that you worked so hard to build. If you throw it out with an awkward exit or with something that doesn't feel natural, you could blow all that hard work you put into connecting, relating, mirroring, and leaving a positive impression. Practice these techniques, make them feel natural and a part of your networking style. These are good starters to practice with if you don't know where to go. Make sure that they feel important still, that your connection is solid. Make sure you let them know you've really enjoyed this conversation.

- *It was great exchanging ideas with you. I'll keep an eye out for anything that I think will help with that current project you were talking about in the aviation realm. I know someone here who'd be fascinated by what you're doing. Is it okay if I introduce you?*
- *I have a few people that I need to meet while I'm here, but I'd love to schedule a call for Monday to continue our conversation. What's your availability like on Monday?*
- *Oh, thanks for sharing your thoughts on this. I want to respect your time too. I know you're here to meet others just like me, but let's catch up soon. Here's my business card.*
- *I'm going to check out some of the other booths over here, but it was wonderful talking to you. Enjoy the rest of the event and don't forget to shoot me an email about XYZ.*

Whatever it is they're doing, their family's doing, their new vacation that's coming up, whatever it is. You can be honest. You do not have to make something up. Make sure whatever you say is you. *Hey, I need to circulate a little more around here, meet a few more people, but this conversation has been one highlight of my day. Thank you so much and here's my business card. Here's my phone number. Call me next week. Let's catch up and talk about how we can get you to XYZ.*

You don't even have to make it about that. You can say, *I'd be interested in hearing more about your design in your new house you're building.* Another good one you can use if you're out of other ones and you don't know where to go. *I'm going to go grab another coffee and refresh myself in the restroom. Can I get you something while I'm up?* They say, no, that's good. Then you close out easily with great. *I'll catch up with you a bit later. Enjoy the next session.* Something like that's not awkward.

Or, *oh, I'm going to run to the restroom. I know we only have a couple of minutes. Well, it's been so great chatting. Send me an email next week. Let's catch up. How about Wednesday? Wednesday work for you?* Nurture that connection. Those are a couple tips on graceful exits.

I hope you've been able to take away a lot of valuable tips that you can start implementing, not only in your networking, but in your daily life when you're meeting people. Start working on building successful connections. You don't have to wait for a summit or a virtual event. You can start networking on social media, the grocery store, the parking lot, your weekend event, or your doctor's office. Start introducing yourself to more people more often and watch how your network grows, not just your network right within your little niche in business, but your network of resources that I know you can learn from and reach out to help others. Remember, the goal is to focus on others.

Mastering Networking for Business Success Conclusion

What a journey we've been on together and as we wrap up this chapter, I want you to take a moment to give yourself a pat on the back. You've come a long way, diving deep into the world of self-confidence, effective feedback, and authentic communication. You've embraced the power of your presence and learned to stand tall, both figuratively and literally, in any room that you enter. Remember the skills and insights that you've gained here. They're not just the key to success in the business world. They are also skills that you could use in your everyday life. Whether it's nailing power poses before a big meeting or before meeting someone new, it's using your authentic voice in every conversation. You're now equipped to convey your message and your brand better than ever. Don't think our journey ends here. The next leg of our adventure lies in mastering marketing. We're about to jump into the dynamic world of marketing where creativity beats strategy, and ideas transform into success stories. Get ready to turn those clicks into customers and remember marketing isn't just about selling products, it's about connecting, engaging, and building relationships. Now that we've talked about building connections, building those authentic relationships, expanding your network, you're ready to move into this next phase in marketing mastery We're going to explore the latest trends, strategies, and Insider tips that will up your marketing game from digital campaigns that make people stop and click to developing messages that stick and resonate with your audience. Whether you're a seasoned pro or dipping your feet in that vast ocean of marketing, this chapter is your ticket to making waves. Gear up, stay excited, and get ready to make your mark in the world of marketing. Together, we're going to turn your vision for your business into your reality, your brand into a sensation, and your dreams into your achievements.

Christy's Trick to Remembering Names Bonus

Ever been in a room full of people and think, how am I going to remember everyone's name? Here's my quick hack that I use. It's not a magic trick, but close enough. When someone says their name, number one, repeat it. Like, so nice to meet you, Mark. If you're able to, like in a meeting, write a brief note. It could be their coffee choice, they love cats, a sports team, anything unique about them. Here's my favorite. Create a silly rhyme. Like when I met Jake at a restaurant expo a couple of weeks ago, and he mentioned he loves to create new cake flavors. *Jake likes to bake cake.* It sounds silly, but trust me, it sticks. Last, snap a mental picture. Like Sarah with the bright blue scarf. Next time you bump into them, you can say, hey, Sarah, rocking another fabulous scarf? Don't forget, names matter. People love it when you remember the little things. Makes you more likable and memorable.

Leverage LinkedIn: A Quick Guide to Business Growth

Want to use LinkedIn to its full potential? This guide is your fast track to mastering LinkedIn for business success. Learn tricks on how to connect with the right people, engage your audience, and grow your business. Whether you're new to LinkedIn or looking to up your digital presence, this guide has you covered with actionable tips and strategies. Let's get your LinkedIn working for you!

http://bit.ly/4d1mJ7f

Chapter 6 Sales and Marketing Mastery Introduction

Imagine this: you have an incredible business, a product you believe in, or a service that can change lives. But here's the million-dollar question: how do you make the world see, believe, and buy into that vision? Welcome to the transformative world of marketing. This chapter isn't just about learning tactics; it's about changing how you approach sales and marketing. We're diving into the core of modern business—digital marketing that grabs attention, brand positioning that makes you unforgettable, customer retention that builds lasting loyalty, and scaling strategies that take your business to new heights. It's not just about transactions; it's about creating a movement, a community, and a legacy. Whether you're a seasoned entrepreneur or just starting out, this chapter is your playground for innovation. We're breaking boundaries, challenging norms, and redefining marketing together. Buckle up for the Marketing Mastery Express—your ticket to not just surviving but thriving in the business world.

The Basics of Marketing Magic

Let's explore the basics of marketing and how it can propel your business to the seven- and eight-figure mark. Marketing isn't just about selling; it's about creating a connection, building a brand, and establishing lasting relationships. Think of it as understanding your customers and speaking directly to them in a way that resonates.

First, remember that resource management is crucial. Use your budget and time wisely, especially if you're a small or mid-sized business looking to soar past eight figures. Next, focus on developing a strong brand identity. Stand out in the crowded market by creating a unique image that differentiates you from competitors.

Knowing your audience is key. Beyond demographics, dive into psychographics to understand your customers' motivations, preferences, and pain points. This is essential for crafting targeted strategies that connect. For instance, if you're selling eco-friendly products, find out what drives environmentally conscious consumers and tailor your message to their values. Remember, effective marketing is about flexibility. Small businesses need to stay nimble, adapt to market shifts, and incorporate customer feedback swiftly. Developing a customer persona helps you identify who you're talking to, so you can craft messages that speak directly to their needs. When it comes to pain points, don't just focus on the problem. Understand the challenges, but center your messaging on the solution. It's about providing exactly what your customers desire, addressing what's eating up their time and money, and making your offer a no-brainer by showing them a clear ROI.

Finally, align with both short-term and long-term goals. Even if selling isn't in the plan, build your business as if it were, creating a scalable and desirable operation. That's how you make a lasting impact and build something truly marketable.

Buying Behaviors and Decision-Making

Understanding your customer's buying behavior is key. What motivates their purchases? What factors influence their decisions? You need to know how they come to their final choice and what drives them to make it. What do they prioritize when making decisions?

Shopping and Communication Preferences

Next, focus on their shopping channels. Do they prefer shopping online, in a store, or through social media? Knowing where they shop most often will help you target them more effectively. Also, consider how they like to communicate. Do they prefer email, phone, social media, or in-person interactions? Everyone has their preferred way of staying in touch. For instance, many clients prefer quick email communication, while others might prefer regular face-to-face meetings, even virtually.

Marketing Engagement

What types of marketing content do they engage with the most? Are they drawn to videos, blogs, webinars, or social media posts? Knowing where and how your audience consumes content will help you create more effective marketing strategies.

Making Their Lives Easier

How can you simplify things for your customers, whether through products, services, or the way they access them? Consider streamlining your purchasing process, offering flexible budget options, or providing personalized support. By understanding their potential hesitations and addressing concerns upfront, you're setting the stage for a smooth sales process. When you're in that sales conversation, remember—it's not a pitch. It's a connection, a conversation. You're there to understand them and offer a no-brainer solution. Make it clear that saying "yes" just makes sense. Present your offer as exactly what they need, solving their problems with an undeniable ROI. It's about speaking directly to them, understanding their unique needs, and presenting your solution as the ideal answer. Stay proactive. Note down any common objections or concerns you anticipate and address them during your conversation. Keep up with evolving market trends, and regularly reassess how your brand is presented. You want customers to feel like your business is always one step ahead, consistently offering them the best solutions. Know who you're speaking to. You can't expect to resonate with your audience if you don't deeply understand them. By focusing on your ideal customer, you can tailor your message to speak directly to their desires, showing them why your solution is perfect for them. Make your approach personal, relevant, and absolutely clear on how you're solving their specific problems. That's where the real magic happens.

Marketing Mastery- Brand Identity

Marketing is more than just selling—it's about clearly conveying who you are and what you do to your ideal client. This starts with brand awareness. A memorable brand comes from a consistent voice and visual style that reflects your unique value and sets you apart. To stay top of mind, we'll focus on building a distinct brand identity that's instantly recognizable. Start by defining your core values, mission, and unique selling proposition. These are the pillars of your brand. Your core values reflect what your business stands for, your mission shows your purpose beyond profit, and your unique selling proposition highlights why customers should choose you over the competition. For instance, a plumbing client I worked with needed to stand out in a saturated market, so we emphasized their unique value to make them memorable. Without a strong brand identity, people will just pick the first name they see online. Brand awareness creates a lasting impression that makes them remember you.

Differentiating yourself also means studying your competitors. Understand what they do well, where they fall short, and how you can offer something unique. It's not about copying; it's about finding your place in the market. To stand out, you need to define your brand persona. Is it friendly, professional, fun, or innovative? Shape a brand story that aligns with your values and mission and can be adapted to different contexts, from a quick elevator pitch to a podcast feature.

Next, develop your brand style. This includes colors, fonts, and imagery that convey the right emotions. Colors carry emotional weight—choose them to match your brand's vibe. For example, we use black and gold at Next Level Connected for a sophisticated feel, while my med spa uses calming blues. Ensure consistency in fonts and imagery across your website, social media, and marketing materials. Your visuals should align with the brand persona and the feeling you want to evoke. Define your brand voice. Is it professional, casual, energetic, or a blend? My voice is conversational yet professional—a tone that resonates with most industries. Keep it simple, engaging, and consistent across all channels. Think of brands like Wendy's, known for their humorous and snarky tone that fits their audience. Whatever voice you choose, ensure it aligns with your industry and audience. For instance, at Next Level Connected, we use an uplifting and motivational tone that inspires businesses to achieve their goals. At Atlanta Bread, our tone is more laid-back and cozy, creating a welcoming space for relaxation or work. Your brand voice should be the same across all platforms, even if the content varies. This consistency builds trust and familiarity with your audience.

Consistency is key not only in branding but also within your team. Everyone brings their unique style, but it should harmonize with the overall brand voice, like different musical notes blending into one song. Regularly gather feedback to understand how your brand is perceived, and adjust to stay relevant. Stay ahead of trends to be the trendsetter, not the follower. Knowing your audience and competitors, and continuously refining your unique angle, will help you connect with your clients on a deeper level. The goal is to drive your business past seven or eight figures by making your brand visible, accessible, and engaging. From building a user-friendly website to mastering social media and email marketing, a solid brand strategy is your ticket to sustainable growth and long-term success. Let's get started!

1. Website Essentials

A user-friendly website is crucial, especially for SEO and brand credibility. Be cautious when getting a quote for your website—it's easy to overspend. For service-based businesses (non-e-commerce), you can build an affordable site. Platforms like Wix or WordPress (with Elementor) make it easy to create a professional-looking site without needing a coder. If you're e-commerce, expect higher costs due to the added functionality needed. Make sure whoever builds your website includes regular updates in their service plan, because a website isn't a onetime deal—it needs consistent maintenance. If you're unsure, reach out to Next Level Connected for a free consultation, and we'll help guide you. For those just starting, there are beginner-friendly options, even some AI tools. While AI can give you a head start with content creation and templates, always put your personal, human touch on it. AI-generated content can't fully capture your brand's unique voice without your input.

2. Using AI Wisely

AI is a fantastic tool for idea generation, research, and speeding up the process of creating content. It can save hours of time by providing outlines and data in seconds. However, AI is only as good as the prompts you give it—generic inputs lead to generic results. Always fine-tune the output to align with your brand's voice and ensure it resonates with your audience.

We at Next Level Connected offer innovative AI solutions that learn your business in 30 seconds, boosting SEO, driving customer engagement, and even acting as a customer service agent. But the key is partnering AI with human expertise for the best results.

3. SEO and Digital Presence

Whether you're service-based or e-commerce, having a digital presence is non-negotiable. Even if you rely heavily on referrals, like one of our HVAC clients, a solid website paired with good SEO can drive more business than you expect. If you're not online, you're not maximizing your potential. Take, for example, a client who owned a commercial upholstery company. Despite relying on word-of-mouth, we built them a website, added AI tools, and implemented digital marketing strategies like SEO and outreach. The result? A 300% increase in sales within the first three weeks.

4. Email Marketing Is Still Alive

Despite what some might say, email marketing is alive and thriving. When done right, it's a powerful way to build connections and drive sales. Think of it as a numbers game—even a small conversion rate can lead to substantial returns. Use emails to share tips, updates, and personalized offers that keep your audience engaged.

When people consider a business, they often start by looking it up—typically on Google or by visiting its website. If they don't find one, it can raise doubts about credibility. A website isn't just about being found; it's about building trust. If you don't have one, don't worry. Start small with platforms like Wix or WordPress. Even AI-driven options are available now. Need more guidance? Reach out—I'm happy to help you figure out what works best for your business.

Tailoring content to each social media platform is crucial. Each channel serves a different purpose and audience. Here's a quick guide:

TikTok is fast-paced, with a focus on quick entertainment and educational tips. Its user base is broadening but still skews younger. Keep it engaging and quick.

LinkedIn is the B2B platform. Share tips, promote your business, and network with other professionals. Content here should reflect your business values.

Facebook is versatile. It's great for behind-the-scenes content, customer testimonials, industry news, and even a touch of controversy (handled respectfully).

Instagram is perfect for brand building and trust through reels and short-form content. Show who you are, not just what you sell.

Twitter is all about quick, punchy updates. Great for spotlighting key points about your business.

YouTube caters to longer content like tutorials and in-depth educational videos, perfect for when people want to dive into a topic.

A content calendar is essential. Plan your week by breaking topics into subtopics for each platform. For instance, one week could include customer testimonials, behind-the-scenes glimpses, and business advice, adjusted for each audience.

Facebook groups are fantastic for networking and collaboration. Share blog links, customer reviews, and behind-the-scenes content to build trust and show the human side of your business. Consistency is vital—post once or twice a day, focusing on quality over quantity. Batch your content creation to streamline the process. Record multiple clips in one sitting, break them up, and schedule them out using tools like Metrical or Hootsuite. This keeps you active without the stress. Aim for a mix of reels, photos, testimonials, and quick takes on trending topics. Whether managing it solo or with a team, consistency is your key to maintaining a steady, engaging presence.

Engagement Tactics

Respond to comments quickly at the beginning to boost engagement. You can use AI chatbots for help, but make sure a real person from your team interacts occasionally with that human touch. People want to feel connected to your brand. Hosting live Q&As or webinars is another great way to engage. You can share snippets on YouTube or stream a podcast. Q&As are especially valuable—they let you hear directly from your audience and help you create content that targets their needs.

Audience-Centered Focus

Always keep your audience in mind. What they want matters more than what you think is interesting. Use feedback from Q&As and polls to guide your content. Check your analytics—look at what gets the most engagement and views. This helps you understand where to focus your efforts moving forward. You can also use tools like ChatGPT to get ideas for trending topics, but always put your unique spin on them. Your goal is to deliver what your audience wants to see and engage with, which helps grow an organic following.

Paid Advertising Options

Consider using Facebook ads to reach a targeted audience. Experiment with formats like carousels, videos, or slideshows. Use Facebook Pixel for tracking and retargeting. For example, you might have 50,000 email subscribers, but if 2,000 people clicked on a specific link, you can re-target that group with content they're more likely to engage with.

Track Performance

Monitor your analytics—monitor what content performs best and adjust your strategy based on real data. This way, you can continuously improve and give your audience more of what they love.

Instagram is all about high-quality visuals and short, punchy captions. Keep it brief—no one wants to read a book on Instagram. Use Stories to give a behind-the-scenes look and reels for tutorials, tips, and product showcases. For example, if you're a restaurant, show off appetizing food videos—like hot coffee with steam rising or a pastry with icing drizzling down. If you're selling a product, show it in action. Make people think, "I need that!" Even if you're B2B, Instagram works for tips, tutorials, and business strategies. Share things like digital marketing advice, sales tips, and business growth hacks—just keep Reels under 60 seconds for maximum attention.

Posting Frequency

Aim for one post per day to start, with a mix of stories and at least three to four main feed posts per week. You can repurpose content from other platforms, but tweak it for Instagram. Consistency is key—keep your audience engaged to avoid losing followers.

Engagement Tactics

Use relevant hashtags to boost discoverability. Think of them like SEO for Instagram—hashtags should match your content. Avoid generic ones like #viral or #FYP; instead, use specific ones like #businessgrowth or #entrepreneurtips. This helps Instagram show your content to the right people. Engage with followers by responding to comments and messages. Prompt replies help build organic connections. People crave interaction, even in a digital world, so show them they matter by answering their questions or highlighting their comments. Make your audience feel valued, and they'll keep coming back.

Collaborating with Influencers and Maximizing Social Media Platforms

Collaborate with influencers relevant to your niche or industry. Engage with them—comment on their posts, support their content, and add your perspective. You don't need to reinvent the wheel. Get inspired by what's trending or what's working for your competitors, then put your unique spin on it, using your brand's voice.

Paid Advertising

You can run Meta-ads on Instagram and Facebook for targeted promotions. Consider sponsored posts with micro-influencers who have an engaged audience. For instance, we partnered with a fitness pro to cross-promote a supplement line, which made sense because the audiences were aligned—fitness and holistic health go hand in hand. Find similar partnerships to introduce your brand to more people, and share their audience while they share yours.

Analytics Monitoring

Use analytics to track engagement and adjust your strategy. Just like Facebook, review insights to understand your audience's behavior and refine your content to better serve their needs.

Twitter Strategy

On Twitter, keep your messages short, impactful, and relevant. Use visuals and videos to increase engagement and respond to industry trends for credibility. Tweet at least once daily and consider hosting Twitter chats on relevant topics. Twitter ads can help drive traffic and leads—just ensure it's the right platform for your audience.

LinkedIn for B2B

LinkedIn is ideal for B2B marketing. Share professional content, company news, industry insights, and thought leadership. Success stories and case studies build credibility. Comment on posts and engage with others to expand your reach. Posting two to four times a week is enough to maintain a professional presence without overwhelming your audience.

TikTok for Engaging Content

TikTok is not just about trends—it's about authenticity. Focus on entertaining, short videos that showcase your brand's personality. Post at least once daily and interact with followers to build a loyal community. You can also collaborate with influencers who align with your target market and use TikTok ads for a wider reach. Remember, people on TikTok want to be entertained and educated quickly, so keep content short and engaging.

General Best Practices

Consistency is key—keep your branding and messaging aligned across all platforms. Tailor your content for each platform's audience, whether it's B2B advice on LinkedIn or entertainment on TikTok. Regularly review your analytics to understand what works and adjust accordingly.

If you use a scheduling tool, many of them have broad analytics built in. You can use that tool to push out content to all platforms for different things, and you can also use that to track your overall analytics in one location. You can consider that as you start to grow and stay updated on each platform's evolving features, trends, and audiences. If you follow these guidelines, you can create a cohesive and effective social media promotion strategy and presence that's going to leverage your strengths and brand. It's going to elevate brand awareness, authority building, credibility building. It's going to help you with your brand identity, and to help you increase leads and generate sales.

Marketing Mastery: SEO for Beginners

Let's start simple. SEO (Search Engine Optimization) isn't as complicated as it sounds, but there are a lot of moving parts. And it's not just about Google anymore. While Google is still a major player, SEO now applies to platforms like YouTube, TikTok, and social media. The goal is to become discoverable and show up in people's searches across all channels. Here's your beginner's guide to SEO, covering the basics without overwhelming you.

SEO is all about making your website, or your content on other platforms, easier for search engines to find, understand, and rank. The better your SEO, the higher you'll appear in search results. Why does that matter? Because most people only look at the first few results on page one. If you're showing up on pages two, three, or beyond, no one's clicking on your site. Ranking high in search results means visibility, traffic, and, ultimately, more business. SEO involves optimizing your website (or social media content) so that search engines like Google can easily recognize and rank it. The key components of SEO include keywords, which are the words or phrases people type into a search engine like *plumber*, *business coaching*, or *digital marketing*. You want these keywords on your site to match what people are searching for.

On-Page SEO: This covers your content, headings, meta tags, and images. It's about making each page on your site clear and valuable for users and search engines. It's more than just keywords—you also need a well-structured, fast-loading website to rank well. SEO is an ongoing process, not a onetime fix. It can take months to see results, which is why I always tell my clients we don't charge until they rank on the first page for the agreed-upon terms.

Backlinks: These are links from other reputable websites that point to your site, showing search engines that your content is credible. The more quality backlinks you have, the better.

Technical SEO: This ensures your website runs smoothly. It covers site speed, mobile responsiveness, and making sure Google can easily crawl (or scan) your site.

Local SEO: For businesses serving specific areas, local SEO is crucial. If you're a local plumber or doctor, optimizing for local searches and managing your Google Business profile can help attract more nearby customers.

To succeed in SEO, you need to understand your audience and competitors. What are people searching for? What's working for your competitors? Then, optimize your website and social media content based on those insights. Remember, SEO is about making your website more visible, relevant, and user-friendly to both search engines and people.

Let's go over the basic steps of SEO:

Keyword Research: Use tools like Google Keyword Planner or Semrush to identify the most relevant keywords for your business. Think of both short-tail (broad terms) and long-tail keywords (specific phrases).

On-Page Optimization: Make sure your meta tags, titles, and descriptions include your main keywords. Use keywords naturally in your website's text—don't stuff them in. Optimize your images with descriptive, keyword-rich file names and alt tags.

Content Creation: Your website should have informative, engaging, and keyword-rich content. This also applies to social media. Add fresh content regularly to stay relevant.

Link Building: Focus on acquiring backlinks from reputable websites in your industry. Quality is more important than quantity—don't just grab links for the sake of it.

Site Speed and Mobile Friendliness: Use tools like Google PageSpeed Insights to improve your website's loading times and ensure it's mobile-friendly.

Crawlability: Make sure search engines can easily crawl and index your website. Use Google Search Console to monitor this.

SEO is a long-term strategy, but when done right, it can drive significant traffic to your site, increase your credibility, and help you reach the next level in your business. It's all about understanding what your audience is searching for and delivering exactly what they need.

Google My Business & Community Engagement

Even if you don't have a website yet, claim and optimize your Google My Business listing. Fill it with accurate information, photos, and keep it updated. Use location-based keywords in your content and get listed in local business directories or review sites like Yelp. Tools like Google Analytics and Search Console can help track your site's traffic, keyword rankings, and user behavior. Regularly check your metrics and refine your SEO strategy based on what's working. SEO is not a onetime thing—it's an ongoing process. Maintaining it consistently will help drive traffic, generate leads, and increase your sales. If you can't handle it yourself, investing in someone to manage it for you is a smart move.

Community Engagement: The Key to Building a Brand

Building a community around your brand—both online and offline—is a powerful way to engage your customers. Whether it's through social media or local events, creating meaningful connections elevates your brand and makes it memorable. Let's dive into both:

Local Community Building:

Host or participate in events that bring people together. For example, if you own a small business, consider hosting events like book readings, knitting clubs, or Coffee with a Cop at local cafes. Even in my restaurant, Atlanta Bread, we host events like these to connect with the community. These gatherings create an opportunity to engage with customers and foster loyalty. You can also partner with local businesses for joint events, offering workshops, seminars, or meetups. For example, at my med spa, we partnered with local gyms to host events. It's a win-win—both of us got access to a wider audience. You can also sponsor local sports teams or organize charity drives, showcasing your brand's commitment to the community while gaining visibility.

Online Community Building:

Create and manage brand-focused groups or forums on platforms like Facebook or LinkedIn. These groups are great places to foster engagement, encourage discussions, and build trust with your audience. Responding to questions and comments creates a sense of belonging for your community members.

User-Generated Content (UGC):

Encourage your customers to share their experiences with your brand on social media. Create specific hashtags for campaigns, feature their content, and show appreciation for their engagement. This builds trust, credibility, and strengthens your community.

Webinars and Live Q&A:

Host webinars, live Q&A Sessions, or online events to connect with your audience. Platforms like Zoom, LinkedIn, and TikTok all have tools to go live and engage with your community. You can also invite industry experts or influencers to draw a larger audience. I often do this on my podcast, where I bring in a variety of experts and influencers to offer diverse perspectives.

VIP and Brand Advocate Groups:

Create exclusive groups for your loyal customers or brand advocates. These groups can get early access to products, exclusive offers, or insider news. Plus, it's a fantastic way to gather feedback before launching a new product.

Pop-Up Events and Sponsorships

If you have a physical location, consider setting up pop-up stores at local festivals or high-traffic areas. For example, we've set up booths at festivals offering pre-made lunch boxes from our bakery. It's a great way to get our brand out there and connect with new customers. You can also sponsor local events or host author readings if you're in a related industry, like a bookstore. These events support local talent while attracting enthusiasts who align with your brand.

Consistency is Key

Whether online or offline, be consistent. Engage regularly, maintain an active social media presence, and always stay true to your brand values. Use tools like Google Analytics or social media metrics to track engagement and refine your strategies. Consistency builds trust, and that trust builds a loyal following.

Adapt Your Strategies:

Marketing isn't a one-and-done deal. Keep tweaking your strategies based on feedback and trends in your industry. Stay in tune with your community, know your competitors, and always be ready to pivot when needed. The most successful businesses are the ones that can adapt to changes and give their audience exactly what they want.

Chapter 7
Sales Systems for Success

Sales aren't just about transactions—they're about relationships, understanding, and strategy. Imagine a sales approach that feels less like a grind and more like an enjoyable conversation with a friend. That's what we're diving into next. We'll explore methods that align with your brand and values, making sales feel natural and authentic, not like a pushy pitch. This chapter will break down how to create a smarter, more effective sales system that truly connects with your customers. These are real, actionable strategies you can start using right away, not just theories or generic advice from social media. By the end of this chapter, you'll see sales from a fresh perspective and be ready to take your approach to the next level.

Tips for Building a Successful Sales System

Let's jump into practical tips to boost your sales and revenue by building a powerful system that works for you.

Tip 1: Understand Your Customer

To sell effectively, you must know your customer. This means building a relationship and nurturing it so that the sale becomes a natural extension of that connection. We've already worked on creating detailed buyer personas, which help us understand our customers' needs, challenges, and desires. Now, it's about refining that understanding. Use tools like surveys, interviews, and analytics from social media, customer reviews, and feedback loops to gather as much information as possible. Don't just listen for what they like or dislike—look for the gaps, the things they aren't saying outright. How can you stand out from the competition by addressing what others are missing?

Tip 2: Effective Communication

Sales are about listening—truly listening. Ask the right questions, then focus entirely on the customer's responses. Active listening means putting yourself in their shoes, feeling what they feel, and understanding their perspective. It's about empathy and observation. Watch for subtle shifts in behavior—body language, facial expressions, eye contact. Are they engaged? Or are they closing off, fidgeting, or looking away? These cues tell you as much as their words do. Reading these signs will help you know when to pivot, when you're losing them, or when you've sparked their interest. Use open-ended questions to draw out as much information as possible, allowing you to fully understand what they need and how to address their concerns.

Tip Three: Building Relationships

Sales aren't just about closing deals—they're about building long-term relationships. That's why we focus on understanding people, listening, and effective communication. When you build trust and rapport with your clients, they become repeat customers and bring referrals. Following up after the sale is key. Many think the job is done once the deal is closed, but great salespeople know the importance of post-sale support, checking in, and nurturing that relationship. Stay in touch with clients through social media, newsletters, and email to keep that connection strong.

Tip Four: Leveraging Technology

Use CRM (Customer Relationship Management) tools to streamline your sales and manage client data efficiently. CRMs store all your customer info—names, emails, phone numbers—making it easy to segment customers (potential, current, and past) and deliver tailored solutions. Long gone are the days of keeping business cards—you want everything in one place for easy access. There are plenty of free and paid CRMs available, so choose one that fits your business size and needs. I use different CRMs across my businesses—like Autotask for IT and GoHighLevel for digital marketing—tailoring tools to meet each business's specific needs. CRM helps track interactions, sales progress, and automate repetitive tasks, which is key to scaling efficiently. Automation isn't about losing the human touch—it's about freeing up time for deeper client engagement.

Tip Five: Creating a Structured Sales Process

A structured sales process boosts efficiency and effectiveness. Develop a step-by-step system that fits your business—prospecting, initial contact, presentations, handling objections, closing, and follow-ups. When I work with clients, one of the first things I do is help them create clear Standard Operating Procedures (SOPs) for sales. Documenting processes is essential for scaling and training new team members. You don't have to reinvent the wheel; take inspiration, but make sure it's customized to your specific business needs. Tailor everything from start to finish to reflect how you want your sales process to operate.

Tip Six: Personalize the Sales Experience

Tailor your sales approach to meet each customer's specific needs and preferences. We all have different buyer personas, and each one requires a unique approach. Use the insights from your CRM, past conversations, and feedback to offer exactly what each customer desires. Personalization leads to more deals and satisfied customers.

Tip Seven: Continuous Learning and Adaptation

The sales world is always evolving. Stay updated with new trends, techniques, and tools. Continuously train yourself and your team on the latest methodologies. Attend workshops, follow industry leaders, and adapt what works for your business. Learning never stops.

Tip Eight: Performance Tracking and Analysis

Measure your sales performance with clear Key Performance Indicators (KPIs). Regularly review data to understand what's working and where improvements are needed. Pivot your strategy as needed to keep up with changing customer needs. It's about long-term growth, not just hitting a onetime goal.

Tip Nine: Upselling and Cross-Selling

Offer additional complementary products or services to increase sales. Know your product range inside out and look for opportunities to provide extra value to customers by solving new problems or removing additional challenges.

Tip Ten: Create a Sales Culture

Foster a positive, motivated sales environment. Encourage success by setting clear goals, providing feedback, and recognizing achievements. Build a diverse team in skills, experience, and age. Customize your approach to each team member, just like with clients. Provide what each individual needs to succeed, whether that's mentorship, recognition, or a clear career path. As leaders, our job is to serve and support our team, helping them deliver on the vision and mission.

When we shift our mindset from thinking like managers to acting as leaders, everything changes. Managers give orders and oversee tasks, but leaders focus on individuals, customizing their approach and support based on each person's unique needs. As business owners and leaders, we must serve and connect with our clients and team members, understanding what they're thinking, feeling, and needing to provide the right resources, guidance, and mentorship for success. This individualized approach helps us build stronger relationships, leading to better results and differentiation from competitors. By setting clear goals, offering regular feedback, and recognizing achievements, you create a positive, success-driven culture within your team. Sales isn't just about numbers; it's about supporting each person to thrive. If someone isn't hitting their sales targets, ask, "How are you doing?" Understand what's going on and adjust your strategy to support them. This approach applies not just to sales teams but to the entire company—everyone should be part of the sales process. Sales are about providing solutions and understanding clients, not just closing deals. By following these principles and refining your approach, you'll develop a powerful sales system that drives success and achieves remarkable growth, both in revenue and as a business. Ultimately, success comes from understanding your clients, colleagues, and team members, and that's how you'll take your business to the next level.

Value-Based Selling

Value-based selling focuses on meeting the customer's specific needs by offering solutions that provide real value. Instead of focusing on features, focus on how those features benefit the customer. Shift the conversation to what your product or service does for them. What problem does it solve? That's what you're selling. To be effective, research your customer's business, industry, and goals. What do they need? What keeps them up at night? Whether it's B2B or B2C, understand their pain points. For example, if you're working with a doctor's office, focus on the result: more patients. You're selling them exactly what they need to solve their problems and reach their goals.

In your first interaction, focus on building a relationship, not a sales pitch. Build trust and rapport, be relatable, and show genuine interest in their needs. Active listening is key. Listen not to respond, but to truly understand their concerns, goals, and challenges. Practice reading body language and subtle behavioral cues to see what resonates with them. Tailor your pitch to their needs and use social proof—examples of how you've helped others with similar challenges. Show them the value of what you're offering, and how it leads to cost savings, increased revenue, or better efficiency. The goal is to eliminate their headaches and make them more profitable. Communicate this value clearly, using data to back up your claims.

Once you've closed the deal, continue fostering the relationship. Provide exceptional service, anticipate their needs, and address concerns. Understand their needs before they do—this builds trust and sets you apart as an expert. For example, one of my real estate clients advised buyers to consider a three-car garage before their children needed a car. This proactive approach made her a trusted advisor and led to more referrals. Value-based selling is about understanding your clients better than they understand themselves and delivering solutions that fit their specific needs. This builds trust, drives referrals, and positions you as an authority in your field.

Another piece, don't forget, is the follow-up in sales. After a sale, remember that's step number one. Now, we need to transition them to whatever piece they need to go to next. Follow up, ensure they're satisfied, continue to address questions and additional needs. This also allows you to cross-sell and upsell. More than that, it shows them you care. You're nurturing that relationship past the sales pitch, and they will feel more connected and more likely to remain with you long-term, which is more likely to create a lifetime customer. Customer retention is necessary because it's less expensive on your part typically to keep a customer or to upsell to that customer than it is to pay for the leads to capture additional customers. Make sure you follow up and use this opportunity to establish a long-term relationship.

Finally, continuous learning and adaptation. Seek feedback often from your team members and customers. Always look for ways to improve and offer better service, products, and a better sales process. Adapt and improve. That's how you remain relevant, stay ahead of trends, and create a sustainable business model. Always use that feedback to refine your offers as the business landscape evolves. Know what your competitors are doing, what's working, what's not, and where the gaps are. Value-based selling: The takeaway is that it's all about putting your customers' needs at the forefront of your sales process. It requires you to fully and deeply understand their challenges, pain points, perspectives, vision, goals, and desires. Building genuine relationships requires focusing on how your services and solutions can add value to their lives and businesses. You need to articulate effectively how you can achieve what they want. How can you achieve higher sales? How can you foster lasting customer loyalty? These are so important for a sustainable business model. Remember that every interaction is an opportunity to learn more about that customer or business, whether B2B or B2C.

Consultative Selling

Consultative selling is based on building trust and understanding what our customers need and want. It positions the salesperson, or us as trusted advisors, rather than salespersons. The client knows you are the expert, and you will be their trusted advisor who will provide them with the exact solution they are looking for.

Let's discuss shifting from a traditional sales pitch to a consultative approach. Traditional selling, or as I call it, the old method, really focuses on pushing a product or a service. You go into that meeting already knowing exactly what you will sell. You know the products and services you offer. You've done your homework, wherein you know that client, what you're going to provide them, but you want to go in there with an open mind and truly understand the customer's needs before you provide a solution. A consultative selling approach will put me in that client's shoes and genuinely looking through their lens, like we discussed, understanding precisely what they want. What are they looking to achieve, and what obstacles are preventing them? I need to fully understand that before I provide a solution. Then, I want to go in and provide the right fit for that client. For example, I recently met with a chiropractor's office, and we were talking about taking over their IT and digital marketing with our business strategy. It was for next-level connectivity, and I went in and really did my homework. I understood a lot of the business. I knew what they were looking to achieve. I understood their ultimate desire, but I wanted to go into this and learn a bit more about what they've done that has or has not worked, what some of the additional challenges might be, and come up with a couple of options. You don't want to give too many options because then you get into analysis paralysis, and they can't decide, but you want to provide them with a couple of options, if possible, to really put them in control. They're in the driver's seat. They're telling you this is what would fit best.

The three options I gave them were custom-tailored to this individual's practice. Go in with an open mind to learn new information and gather as much data as possible before you present what you want to show. That does a couple of things. Number one, it gives you more insight and leverages that understanding to sell more efficiently. Number two, it arms you with precisely what you need to lay out the product or service in a fashion that is most appealing to that client, showing them why it's the missing puzzle piece. Think of your role as more of a consultant than a salesperson, and in building that foundation, you want to understand the ins and outs of that industry, that product, the customer needs, and the challenges. Ensure you stay updated on industry trends and all the new pieces of information about how your product or service is the missing piece in this market. Keep abreast of challenges, innovations, and competitors. In this approach, you want to use a lot of active listening. Make it a rule to listen more than you speak. Understand the client's situation, pain points, challenges, and ultimate goals and desires. You can practice active listening techniques with someone at home, a friend, or a colleague. Incorporate nodding, not an excessive amount, but when it's appropriate. Remember that a nod can indicate continuing. Ensure you're summarizing throughout so that if there is something you misunderstood, it can be clarified there before you present the wrong solution. Ask follow-up questions. Before showing a solution, you want to fully listen, understand, and confirm you understand. Ask all the questions you need, learn all the information you need, and now you are a consultant. You are their trusted advisor. You are here to remove the challenges and get them to their ultimate desire. That's more than a consultative sales approach. When you ask questions, you make them open-ended as applicable, which encourages them to express more needs and challenges. You would not believe what you learn when you ask a couple of questions and let somebody else talk. You'll learn a ton about that business or that customer. Tailor your questions based on your preliminary research. Then you can pivot throughout that conversation and ask questions based on what you're hearing and what the client is providing you with.

Make sure that your pitch is personalized. Your solution should match exactly what this customer is looking to achieve, and it should remove the challenges, obstacles, and pain points surrounding the desired result. Show how your product or service can address their unique challenge.

This is a solution-based presentation. You are a consultant, an advisor. You will present your product or service as a solution to their specific product and focus on the benefits and outcomes, not just features. It's okay to discuss features when discussing how this benefits and leads to their ultimate desire or outcome. Remember, building trust and credibility is critical. You cannot sell or be a trusted advisor if they don't trust you, so you need to establish that connection and trust early on using methods we've discussed earlier. You also want to make sure you're consistent in your message. We talked about building a brand with consistent messaging, so you have credibility. You're educating your customers on the potential solution, even if they don't directly involve your product. You are there to solve their problem, not to sell. This approach positions you as their trusted advisor. This type of selling approach is about building trust and long-term relationships. That way, you can keep in touch with the customer after the sale, providing ongoing support, advice, and resources. Even if they don't end up accepting the sale, you now have that bond of trust, and you don't know where that will lead down the road. You can come in later and present the solution to something else you discover during your discussion. It requires continuous learning, regularly updating your knowledge and skills, following industry leaders, and knowing everything about what you're selling to be that trusted advisor. Then, to measure success, as always, you can track your progress using your CRM. You can monitor metrics like client satisfaction, repeat business, and referral rates. Studies have shown that people prefer consultative selling. It's about understanding your customers, providing custom-tailored solutions, and building lasting relationships. Remember, it's about relationships, connections, and people.

Your business will succeed because of people. If you implement these steps and continuously refine your consultative approach, you'll meet your sales targets and exceed them. You'll become an indispensable resource and knowledge expert to your clients with a long-term relationship. Remember, retention is cheaper than new leads. We want to keep those customers, and you could cross-sell, upsell, or get a referral. The key is to position yourself as a knowledge partner. It's a genuinely invested partnership in your client's success. If you're offering them a product or service, you should be genuinely interested in and invested in your client's success. Remember, we shift the focus to others. How can we serve them? That's going to give them the ultimate experience. It will increase your sales, revenue, and profit.

Social Selling

Social selling involves using social media networks to find, connect with, understand, and nurture sales prospects. It's a modern way to develop meaningful relationships with potential customers. When I'm working with a client, one of the first steps in social selling is always choosing the right platforms. You may want to select more than one, but different platforms attract different audiences for various reasons. Now, the same audience can be present on many platforms. Often, they will go to that platform to seek a specific method of communication and a particular input of the content. They like certain styles and certain presentations. Make sure that you're connecting with individuals on the platform that makes sense for what you're selling.

The first step is to identify where your prospects are. Each platform will attract different demographics and psychographics; even if it attracts the same audience, they come to that platform for various reasons. For example, LinkedIn is great for business-to-business selling, while Instagram and Facebook are better for business-to-consumer. TikTok has a lot of business-to-consumer, but there's also B2B and some overlap, so I don't want you to limit yourself to one platform. I want you to focus the beginning efforts on the platform that makes the most sense for you and will be most successful. Research where your target audience spends their time. Next, you want to ensure you have a professional online presence within that platform. That means optimizing your profile. We want to ensure that your social media profiles are number one, professional, number two, they're up to date, and number three, that they reflect your brand identity. We discussed the consistency of messaging and having that consistent identity recognizable across different communication methods and channels. This is no exception to the rule. Your profile should clearly state what you do and how you can help potential customers because otherwise, they'll scroll by and think, oh, there's nothing for me here. We want to make sure that we say, *hey, we're over here. We will do this for you.* We want to target them and ensure that we share valuable content on that platform.

If you're on TikTok, it's more entertaining along with educational. Most of LinkedIn will be academic, insightful, and motivational, something that will assist other businesses. Ensure that when you're planning your content strategy, you are sharing insightful and valuable content relevant to that specific audience. That's who you're looking to target, your ideal customer. This can include anything from articles to blog posts, infographics, stories, reels, and videos. Appear consistent and stay in their minds. The more somebody sees somebody or a brand, the more trust is built, and the more it's locked into their memory. They say the average person needs at least three to four touchpoints before considering buying from a brand or a person. That's the majority, and some say it can take seven to 11 different touchpoints to connect with that brand and build trust. Keep that in mind when we talk about regular content posting, and you want to ensure that you're positioning yourself or your brand as a thought leader in your field. Because who do we want to buy from? We want to buy from the expert. If you don't know what you're talking about, haven't done this, or can't showcase why you're a thought leader in this area, I'm going to go over here to this person who clearly knows more about it. We must position ourselves as a thought leader for that brand's authority.

Next is engaging with your audience. Like, comment on, share posts, share posts from others, and like other posts, especially those of people in your industry or potential customers. You can also follow competitors. It keeps you up to date on everything they're doing. Remember, we want to know our competitors well, just like our customers. You also want to follow customers. You can form a Facebook or LinkedIn group that attracts an ideal client. You can be a thought leader among your colleagues and competitors. It's also an excellent place to meet people with whom you can collaborate or partner. When you have similar interests that align with your audience, your interests will overlap, but you will offer different services or products. Join relevant groups and forums, participate in the discussions, and get your brand out there. Then you can build and nurture relationships. You can send personalized requests and connection requests to potential leads. You can mention something that you have in common or in a recent post of theirs that you found interesting. They've already seen your name and comments, and there's that bit of trust that's already started, that familiarity, and people like or gravitate toward familiarity. You want that connection, and you've already built it. Now, you can send them a personalized message and connect over something they posted. That's another reason we want to expand, like, and comment on other posts. My recommendation is not to pitch immediately. When we connect, we are focused on building a relationship because people buy from people they trust and brands they trust that are well known, that they're a leader in that industry, and that they know what they're talking about. They're experts, and we have a connection, a bond. There are some similarities. There's familiarity. When they start to feel comfortable, they'll start looking into the products and services. You want to use what I like to call social listening. It sounds weird. Social listening, monitoring conversations, using tools to listen to what people are saying about your industry, your brand, or relevant topics within that industry, and engaging in the conversation where you can provide value. You can use tools like answerthepeople.com. You can ask a question or put in keywords, and answerthepeople.com will give some of the most asked questions that people are searching for within that industry, trend, and keyword. You can do that several times a day for free. There are paid subscriptions for advanced features. But if you're looking for something to start with, you can do that for free.

Listen to competitors on social media. Don't reinvent the wheel; see what's trending. What are people talking about? Keep your ear to the ground. Then you'll be able to engage in those conversations with insightful, educated answers, and you'll remain a trusted advisor in that industry. You're a knowledge expert. You'll want to measure your success. Using analytics, KPIs, and social media platforms today has made it very easy. Many of them have excellent free analytics built into them. You can also use a scheduling tool. I use Metricool, but you can use any of them. Many of them have free versions. If you need a subscription, some are inexpensive, and offer more advanced analytics. Use those analytics, tools, and your CRM to measure the effectiveness of your social selling efforts. Track metrics within the platform, like engagement rates, the number of leads generated, and conversion rates. That's going to be very important to understand whether your content or approach is resonating or whether you found your ideal audience and cost. You need to know how many leads you've generated and your conversion rate to see if you're getting your ROI, if you're paying for ads, and if you're paying for resource time. Allocate that to the proper category so you can accurately calculate the cost of a lead here. Is it a time cost and does that equate to a money cost? What is the cost? Then, you want to adapt and stay informed. Continuous learning applies here. Keep up with the latest trends in social media, sales techniques, and what people are looking for, what resonates with them, what's working, and what isn't. Then, adapt your strategy. As social media platform behavior changes, we must evolve our strategy to match the trend.

We want to give people what they want. Remember, it's about others. Adapt your approach. If you're going to do this yourself, I'd recommend setting aside a specific time each day for those social selling activities. You don't want to get wrapped up where you spend your entire day doing that, but you also want to block it out, so you don't forget, or it doesn't slip by. It's essential to remain consistent. That includes posting your content and recording, and I always recommend batch recording. When I do mine 99% of the time I batch record. What that means is I sit down, I have a topic; I break it into little subtopics, and I talk a little about each one. Earlier today, I took part in a media interview. I recorded that myself. I'll have my team chop that up and utilize it for YouTube shorts. I can use certain pieces for LinkedIn. I can highlight the other partner there, and the other collaborator, tag them, and tap into their audience, the media's audience, and my own.

If that's overwhelming, you can start on only one platform. Reach out if you have trouble, and I'll give you more personalized advice. Then, you can also outsource this as you grow larger, and it makes more sense. I run an entire organization with a social selling and digital marketing division. It can use a specific platform or program to help you shorten the time you must put into it as it grows. Start simple. If you're starting yourself, start on one platform, optimize that, and then expand from there. I'd recommend, especially as you're building your name and brand, always maintain a personal and human touch in your interactions. People want to connect with people, not just a brand, not just a business, and not just a bot. You can use those tools. They are powerful help for business owners today, but you don't want to rely on them solely. I keep that in mind when I'm recording, even though I use that program; I also have team members that check things. I look at comments to make sure that I'm responding appropriately and that it's responding appropriately. Sometimes, I sit down here, start talking, and chop it up. Sometimes, I record deliberate, short pieces of content.

Keep that connection with your customers. Make sure that they know you. They feel it's familiar, and that's where you'll be successful in the social selling scene. Like everything else, building relationships is essential. Your business' success depends on people. Build a robust and fantastic team. They will help you build a tremendous company. Keep your ear to the ground and understand them inside and out. Look at things through your customer's lens. Put yourself in their shoes. Understand where their frustrations lie. Understand what they want so you can give them exactly what they want. Always nurture and aim to grow your network, whether here, on social media platforms, or in person, preferably both. I like holistic approaches, variety, and diversification. People are your business, so shift your focus to others. How can I serve others, my team, clients, and my network? It'll return tenfold. Social selling will be important in any business. I know many people say, "Oh, I don't need social media for my type of business." Everybody needs social selling online. It requires strategy, consistency, and a humanized personal connection. Try these tips and reach out.

Inbound Selling

Leave behind the notion that it's this used car salesman pitch. No offense, but the old methods of selling don't work. They're not what people want. They want trusted advisors and consultative selling. Let's discuss how we can attract customers by aligning with buyer behavior. Forget the old-school tactics. It's time to pull customers in with actual value and knowledge. What is inbound selling? Inbound selling is a method that aligns with modern consumers' purchasing decisions. What does that mean? Unlike traditional sales methods, which involve reaching out to potential customers through cold calls, emails, and snail mail, inbound selling will focus on attracting those customers through valuable content and interactions. Let's break that down. I recommend a holistic or tailored approach based on what works in your industry, your ideal audience, and your needs. I use a mix of everything based on the business. Before I sold my med spa, I used direct mail. I also used inbound selling, cold calls, emails, ads, and social selling. Sometimes, it's a combo approach. I do not use direct mail with Next Level connections, but I use emails and cold calls. I use inbound selling and social selling, along with consultative selling.

Let's discuss inbound selling. It's not just a strategy; it's a mindset shift. It's about understanding that today's buyers are savvier, informed, and want value. They're not waiting for us to come and sell to them. They're out there actively searching for solutions for themselves. You're saying, well, what's our job? Our job is to be the beacon that guides them to the right answers. Say you're searching for a new CRM system. You will not wait for a sales call. You need it today. You thought I had better start researching CRMs. Where'd you go? Did you sit by your telephone and wait for the call? Of course not. You went to Google. That's what inbound selling is all about. You didn't wait by your phone for somebody to cold call you or for a mailer to find out what CRM would be a good fit for your business. You went out, searched, became informed, and became more knowledgeable. Now you have some knowledge going into this. That gives you that feeling of a bit of control. We all like a little control, some of us more than others. We enjoy having a choice. With inbound selling, content is like your handshake. If you're looking at the old sales process, inbound selling is that initial handshake. It's your conversation starter and how you build trust and show your expertise as a brand. Create content that educates your audience—blog posts, webinars, ebooks, anything that answers their questions. Remember, we talked about how to identify and find out what their questions are. We can use tools such as answerthepublic.com. There's a lot out there to discover the common questions within the industry.

That's why we want to stay current on the trend and create content that efficiently educates our audience. We want them to come in and feel they're knowledgeable. They know what this is. They're in control, and they have a choice. You don't have to do all these to start, but variety is excellent. If you can publish a blog post, host a webinar on Facebook Live or TikTok Live, maybe you'll put some YouTube content out there. You write up a quick ebook with checklists in it. Anything that's going to help you answer the questions that you're going to research proactively, so you know what to answer. Show don't tell. That's a key there. Use case studies and examples to show how you've solved this problem. Let your success stories do the talking. "Christy, I'm brand new. I'm just starting my business." You started it because you have expertise in a particular area or a team with expertise. Show you can solve the problem by showing how you've done it before. Remember, it could work for me if it worked for them. Like everything else we talk about, consistency is critical. Regularly update your content. Provide relevant, up-to-date content, and be an expert in your field. Stand out from the sea of competition and stay at the forefront of their minds.

Let's explore the psychology behind inbound selling. As we mentioned, it's all about making the buyer feel in control. We might be a control freak, a little Type A. When our customers find us, it's their choice, and that's powerful. When people feel they've discovered you, it empowers them. It's their decision. That will build a stronger connection, build that trust early on, and make them feel like I have an expert in this field. I found them; I researched, and I found them. You also want to ensure that your content creates desire, not just interest. You're wondering how, by tapping into their ultimate goals and desires, understanding their pain points, and offering a solution. Remember, we talked about serving up their ultimate desire on a silver platter? That's what we do when we sell. We offer them precisely what it is they're looking for. We want to create desire, not just pique their interest. Piquing their interest is excellent in the beginning to get their attention. But when you're creating that content that you're going to use for inbound selling, you want to create a desire of *I need that*. That takes away all my pain points and headaches and gets me to exactly where I want to be. How do we make inbound selling work for us? That's the big question. Let's start with SEO. We touched on some of these pieces earlier because optimizing your content for search engines will allow you to be one of the first answers they find. People do not have long attention spans anymore. What do we do? We go to Google. We look at the first two, three, four, and then move on. SEO is your friend and helps people find you on Google. Engage on social media. That's the second key. Don't just post; engage. Comment, connect, respond, like, and answer questions. Look at other competitors' comments on their posts and see what questions are being asked there and then post an insightful answer or response with your own perspective attached to that question.

The third key is personalizing your approach. Use data, as much information as you can gather, to personalize your interactions. Make every email and call feel tailored to that person. You are speaking to one person—your ideal client. Make every interaction count and feel personalized. You can add a personal touch, even if it's dry information, make that connection. Refine your skills in making those connections, build trust, establish brand authority, consistency, and consistent messaging, and have your why, core values, and differentiating edge. Now, we tie all of that together. We gather and personalize our data to make that person feel we are talking right to them, giving them precisely what they desire. Remember, in inbound selling, we're not chasing but attracting. We're pulling them to us. We're not interrupting, not calling up during dinner, and interrupting on a cold call; we're engaging. We're a trusted advisor. Be authentic in this. When you are selling your product or service and training your team to sell your product or service, we don't want to chase, interrupt, or sell. That old method of selling, throw it out in the trash. We are attracting, pulling people to us, and getting their attention. We're engaging with them, connecting, learning, and reading that person to understand their desire and why they can't get what they want. Then we're helping. We are giving them the solution to rid them of what's holding them back from reaching their goal and desire. Your goal is to help others. Remember, we talked about successful businesses, sales, marketing, and anything in business is about people. People are your business, from your team to your customers to your network. CEOs today, business owners, and entrepreneurs get so wrapped up in things that we forget that vital key: What is our business? It's people. I don't care what you do; it's people. You're serving your team by providing them with the support, career paths, growth, mentorship, environment, and culture they want to be a part of. You're giving them a vision, something they can share. Many diverse notes make up that one voice, one vision, and one mission. You're serving your customers. You are developing custom-tailored products and services to help them, ridding them of the pain points and problems and getting them to where they need to be. Your network should be focused on making genuine connections. You'll get a lot out of networking, but your focus should be on what you can do to help others. Share your challenges, how you overcame them, and your successes. More importantly, share your failures so they can learn from them and don't have to make the same mistakes you did. Your business is people. We're not chasing, interrupting, or selling to them. We attract, engage, and connect with them—a valuable, genuine connection. Practice what we've discussed. Write down your goals, break them into baby steps, and start doing little things that help align you and your brand with your ideal customers.

Account-Based Selling

I nicknamed Account-Based Selling, ABS. What is ABS? It's a strategy that may or may not apply to your business. You must determine which strategy, or strategies, make the most sense and align with your business goals and ideal customers. Think of ABS as every pitch you make. Every pitch you make is like a perfectly cut key to fit the exact lock of high-value clients. Account-based selling means focusing on a few high-value accounts rather than a quantity of lower-value accounts. In this method, looking at it as forging a lasting partnership is essential. You're not a vendor; you're a partner. That should be your mindset. For example, I had a client a couple of years back. They were a small tech startup that offered software as a service. They transformed their entire sales approach with account-based selling. They had this potential client who seemed out of reach, beyond what they could do. Instead of casting a wide net to capture a lot of fish, they focused on understanding this client's unique challenges and goals. They tailored every interaction and every piece of content to this specific client. Guess what? The big fish didn't just bite; they became a client for the tech company and a loyal advocate for them. The secret of account-based selling is simple. It's understanding the specific needs of high-value accounts and targeting everything in that niche. You'll only focus on a few, but they'll be high value. This primarily works well with B2B, especially when you're starting up. I will rewind to 2016 when I launched WOOS IT. It's now a part of Next Level Connected, a whole division. Back then, we had very few resources. It was my husband, Josh, and me. We were the company. Instead of casting a wide net and going after all sizes, we focused on one niche. We started with chiropractors. From there, we were off and running and had to pivot and change our sales approach. We no longer use just ABS, but we go after a diverse group of clients, and we now have people in almost every industry, A to Z, and we have a team. We were limited in resources when it was just us.

Going after a lot, we really didn't have the funds to support bringing on a team and scaling up before we had the clients. We used the ABS approach, and that's where we focused in the chiropractor world only back then. Within the first 30-ish days, we had signed on three multi-practice locations. They were high value, with a higher retainer per month, and we were doing just IT back then—all technology, security systems, et cetera. We brought them on, and then we transitioned. We focused on that targeted approach, fewer but higher-value accounts, and it made sense because Josh and I could handle that with the two of us rather than needing a team. Then, we took what we made there, reinvested in scaling, and built the team so we could diversify and grow. We took WOOS IT from zero to seven figures in less than 20 months, and we didn't spend a dime on marketing. It was all network-based referrals. Focus on the few but higher value. Quality over quantity in this method. It doesn't work for everyone. You must determine what aligns with your business goals, the niche, and industry you serve, and what makes sense to you. Just like we tell our clients that it should be a customized approach, that's the same approach you should take in your business. If you want to implement the fundamental principles of account-based selling, you can implement it in one division. I have a more minor division, and when we launch, sometimes we do an account-based selling approach and then pivot from there. The first key principle is the targeted approach. It should target a few but high value.

The second key is personalized communication. Every email, phone call, everything you do should address the client's unique, individualized needs and address their specific pain points.

The third key is team collaboration. That means sales, marketing, customer service, and everyone you involve. Whether you outsource or the two of you do all those pieces, it doesn't matter. Everyone's aligned, working together strategically to win and keep these accounts. What's great about ABS? There's a deeper relationship. You're not just a vendor. You're a trusted partner, advisor, and expert in their business. Another benefit is increased customer lifetime value. Long-term relationships mean sustained revenue for you and better results for your client, building a larger lifetime value with those customers. Third, of course, is higher ROI. Focused efforts on crucial accounts lead to a higher return, which you can reinvest and choose whether to continue account-based selling or use other methods. How do you make ABS work if you're a B2B? First, research is key. Know your high-value clients or accounts inside and out. What are their goals, challenges, and industry trends? You should already know your ideal client inside and out, but it's even more critical in account-based selling. Customized solutions are your second item. Develop solutions that cater specifically to their individualized needs. Third, consistency, consistent engagement, regular check-ins, frequent updates, and valuable insights. Keep that relationship fresh and meaningful.

Now, fast-forward a few years; we have thousands of clients within the IT division, but whether you use an account-based selling approach or not, the principle of ABS should remain a thing in every business. Remember to think about how you can tailor your approach to each client's specific needs. How can you turn a sales relationship into a true partnership? I have a veterinarian who joined in 2017. It's just her, a solopreneur. We have supported her technology needs since 2017, and she still calls us. I ensure that every client we bring on has access to me or Josh. Every client, even my little solopreneur vet down the road, should always feel like they are in the VIP circle. That's how to keep your clients. These strategies can apply to your business, even if you do not use an account-based selling approach. Treat every client like they are in the VIP circle. That is how you create a fabulous experience that makes them never want to leave and sets you apart from your competitors. When people feel valued and like somebody special, they don't want to leave. If I am treated like a VIP somewhere, I typically keep my business there, even when other competitors come in lower priced. *No, I've been with so-and-so forever, and they treat me like a VIP. They answer my calls at 8 p.m.* That's how to build long-lasting client relationships. Treat every account as if you were looking at ABS as your sales approach.

The next session will focus on AI and sales. I love AI. It is not a replacement for people, ever. It's not a replacement for a job, but it accentuates our team's talent. It is a powerful assistant. I was working in AI years ago when we called it machine learning. I led the teams that programmed machine learning, especially within the call center world. We use it. I have this fantastic little AI guy. NLC is his name. He goes onto our client's website, learns their business inside and out, all their social platforms, Google profiles, everything about them that's up there in 30 seconds-ish, and then provides strategy, optimizes SEO, creates content, solicits reviews, and interacts with people and sounds humanized. However, it's still not a replacement for humans. Always keep that human touch. Although it is a powerful assistive tool, it is only as good as the prompt you give it. I'm excited to discuss how we can leverage that and use it as a powerful tool in our business. You should, too, even if you say, *I don't like AI; I'm not good with technology.* Everybody can learn what programs to use that are best for their business. There are so many AI-driven tools out there today, and if you're not using that or not utilizing that, you're missing out on an opportunity. Treat every business as your own and make it a true partnership, because your success is theirs. It's a circle. Their success is your success. That's your testimonial; that's your long-term customer. Retention is cheaper than new leads, number one. You want them to be successful.

AI in Sales

AI-powered tools don't just enhance sales efficiency, they revolutionize the way we connect with our customers. Let's look at some examples here to start AI. You hear about it. It's not a buzzword. It won't slow down or revert. If you've said, *I'm just not technical enough; I'm not tech savvy*. Throw that notion away. You and your team can be trained on tools that utilize AI in your business as a powerful enhancer. It's not a replacement. It's a fabulous assistant. I remember working with a client struggling to keep up with their expanding customer base. They were losing the personal touch they had in their early success. We discussed how vital personal connection is and how to treat every client like a VIP as if they were in the VIP circle. They introduced some AI-powered tools into their sales process. It was a seamless, efficient, connected opportunity to each customer's unique needs. AI is not just about numbers. It's not just plugging it in to run analytics and spit out reports. It's about helping us dive deeper into customer behavior and understand their needs and preferences on a deeper level. We can use that tool to learn and gain insights into our customers. Before, it would have taken us hours to dig up the data, but now, with AI, it streamlines and optimizes, not to replace, but to help our team be more productive. It does things quicker and simpler. You can automate a lot of tasks now.

Some benefits: AI tools analyze data and provide insights into customer preferences. This will help you tailor your approach to that specific customer. You can free up time. Your team can focus on precisely what you do best: building relationships, being the human in the relationship, connecting, nurturing those relationships, getting out there, and networking. This is going to free up your backend time. It also allows you to offer a personalized experience to every customer, no matter how large your client base grows. How do we make this a part of your business? The first thing is that if you're getting into AI, it will be overwhelming. Choose the right tools. Identify tools that align with your specific sales process, whether it's a CRM integration or a chatbot. You need that to interact with customers when you're not available, especially if you're a solopreneur. You could work with predictive analytics. As you grow, train your team, and ensure that they are well-trained to use the tools. Knowledge is power, especially with technology. Even if you're not tech-savvy, there are many free resources, like YouTube tutorials. AI can help by answering questions. Sometimes I get into Word or Excel, and I'm doing something with a formula, and I cannot remember how to set that up. I'll go to ChatGPT and punch in my question. There is a quick step-by-step that I can use. You can even ask AI tools about AI tools. AI is a powerful piece to add to your business.

The next step is to monitor and adapt as necessary. Monitor the performance of the tools you choose and adapt, changing your strategies, pivoting, and adjusting based on the insights you gain. There is nothing wrong with dabbling and trying tools. You don't want to keep trying tool after tool, but there's nothing wrong with finding out that this tool is not exactly what you need or that another tool has emerged that fits your business better. Keep lists and metrics, and analyze, analyze, analyze. We should constantly analyze everything we can to improve our business. That's how we build sustainable companies that scale quickly. They get you past those seven or eight figures and beyond. Chatbots are okay when you can't be available. Make sure that you still have your brand messaging, core values, and that humanized touch when making those connections, but you can use an AI-driven chatbot on a website. I use it with my clients. We have a fabulous tool, a little LLC, out there. He's efficient, and his programming is humanized. He's never going to sub out for a human. These chatbots can provide what people want. What do they want? They have short attention spans and want instant. You can give that instant response. You can personalize it to your brand and answer questions when you're not available. We put this on another client's website less than two weeks ago. It was fantastic. This medical practice has already seen a 30% increase in customer satisfaction and a massive boost in patients and sales of their supplements. Remember, the goal of AI is not to replace the human touch. It's to enhance it. That's the important takeaway.

Now, you need to weigh the pros and cons. I'm going to throw some AI sales tools out here. The first is going to be your CRM systems. You can leverage an AI-enhanced CRM system to track customer interactions, predict your customer needs, and provide personalized recommendations. You can also use predictive analytics to identify potential sales opportunities that might be out there. I would encourage you to look at some CRM systems that have AI capability. Another big one is chatbots and virtual assistants, which I recommend. You can optimize somebody's time with things like Drift Intercom. I'm not endorsing any of these, but I use some of them. These are just things that you can research. You can implement chatbots on your website and social media platforms, and they'll provide instant customer support, qualify leads, and schedule meetings on your behalf. You can use these to answer FAQs, which saves you time. They also allow you to gather preliminary information from sales prospects. Look into it and see which ones you like. Another tool I recommend is email automation tools. You know the big ones, like MailChimp. You can use them for personalized communication at scale. This will help you segment your audience and send targeted messages based on customer behaviors and preferences. Segmenting is one key to email marketing.

Another thing we can use AI for is predictive analytics. You can use predictive analytics tools to analyze your sales data and forecast future trends. That allows you to make informed decisions, so you know which leads to pursue and how to allocate your resources efficiently. There are many lead-scoring software options out there now. You can use this to prioritize your leads based on their likelihood of conversion. You can then focus your efforts on the high-potential prospects to maximize your sales efficiency. You can use some AI-powered social media tools to analyze your social media conversations and understand market trends to engage with customers on social media platforms effectively. You know where to go, who's interacting with what, and what to give them. It helps you identify precisely what they want and how to interact, what times to interact, what content to produce, and what produced well. Another one is sales forecasting tools. You can implement forecasting tools to gain insights into your sales pipeline. Use them for strategic planning and resource allocation.

Make sure you choose tools that align with your goals and objectives. Is it the most effective for what you need in your business? Ensure that the AI tools integrate seamlessly with your existing systems. If you're not changing systems, you want to make sure that those tools complement and are not a hindrance. For example, if the AI tool does not integrate with your CRM and/or marketing automation software, you will not have a streamlined process. It will cost you time and money. Make sure there's a seamless integration there. Then, ensure you conduct comprehensive training for your team and yourself. Make sure that whoever's using it is proficient in using the tools. Make sure that you are gaining efficiency and time and that there's a return on your investment. Then, you want to use the data and insights that you gather from these tools to make informed decisions and personalized sales strategies. Don't get the tool because it's super cool without utilizing the data that you extract from it. Whatever you gain from it, you want to implement. Make sure there's execution, not just putting the tool into place and checking the box. Make sure that there's a good return on your investment. Then, like any other process in your business, regularly evaluate and adjust as necessary. Monitor the performance. Adjust as needed. Stay updated on new features and capabilities to ensure that you maximize their effectiveness. Also, analyze what else exists to ensure this tool is still best aligned with your business goals and objectives.

Finally, focus on customer experience. Use AI tools to enhance the customer experience at every touch point. While you're becoming more efficient by using technology, make sure the human element in the sales interaction is preserved. Leveraging AI sales tools effectively and integrating them into your business processes will significantly enhance your sales efficiency. It will also provide you with more personalized customer experiences and allow you to better meet your customers' needs. Ultimately, that will lead to driving more sales, revenue, and profits for you, pushing you closer to seven, eight figures, and beyond. If you have questions, I will help you in any way I can.

Sales Systems for Success Conclusion

Can you believe that we're already at the end of our chapter? Hopefully, you've been having fun. We've really navigated the ins and outs of sales systems, gone over what a CRM system is, why you want that, and dabbled a little in the art of sales automation. Hopefully, these are strategies you can start implementing immediately into your business. You'll be able to take these tools and strategies and adjust them to make them your own. That's what this is all about. Connecting with your customers that feel genuine and, most important, work for you and your business because every business is unique. Every business strategy should be customized to make it work for you, your core values, your business model, and your goals.

We're about to take things up a notch in our next chapter, Operational Efficiency, and Innovation. If you thought sales systems were exciting, just wait until we dive into making every part of your business run like a well-oiled machine. I know you're thinking, *well, this is about taking my business to seven or eight figures.* It is. But to maintain that and to continue to be scalable, we need to be efficient, innovative, and we need strategies that keep your business thriving successfully and growing consistently. We're going to explore everything from streamlining operations to embracing innovative ways of thinking about how you structure your business for efficiency. This is where your business gets that extra edge, and you see the bigger picture and all the amazing possibilities that lie ahead.

Chapter 8 Operational Efficiency and Innovation

We will dive into a realm where the magic happens behind the scenes, but it drives the entire show. Welcome to Operational Efficiency and Innovation. Imagine a well-oiled machine, each part working in perfect harmony, delivering results beyond expectations. That's what operational efficiency is all about. But how do we get there? More importantly, how do we keep innovating to stay ahead in this fast-paced business world? Now, picture a world where every process in your business will flow as smoothly as an open highway with no traffic jams. Innovation is not a buzzword. It's a daily practice and a mentality within your team. That's where we're headed together in this chapter, from startups to the strategy room of Fortune 500 companies.

Operational efficiency and innovation are the silent drivers behind the scenes. They cut costs, save time, and open doors to unimaginable growth. But here's the real question. How do you embed these into the DNA of your business? In the following few sections, we'll unravel the secret. We'll see how process optimization isn't just about cutting out the fat. It's about making room for more muscle within your business for growth. We'll explore how leveraging technology is about empowering your team to achieve more with less. We're going to discover how to foster a culture that celebrates innovation. I hope you're ready to transform your business, prepared to be the architect of a future where efficiency and innovation drive your business past those seven—and eight-figure marks. We will not adapt to change. We will be the change.

Introduction to Operational Efficiency and Innovation

Operational efficiency is going to be the backbone of your business. It's what goes on behind the scenes that ensures you're operating efficiently, meaning you save money where you need to and spend money on things that lead to growth. Remember, although the goal is to shatter the seven-figure or eight-figure ceiling, it also ensures you are profitable. One thing we must look at is what's our ROI, our return on investment? You can make $100 million, but what did you net after you generated $100 million? When I look at a division to see if we should continue it, I look at what we generate revenue-wise and our net profit. Is it generating a return? If I make $10,000, I want to ensure that I'm not spending $10,000 in overhead and expenses on that project unless it's reinvesting to grow. Operations are like the machinery that powers the business. It will be essential for scaling your business past seven or eight figures. You will not put the complete picture together if you only have one piece of the puzzle. It's the same when striving towards seven, eight figures, and beyond. Without all the pieces of the puzzle, you can't get there. Let's discuss some core principles we will break down for operational efficiency and innovation.

The first thing we want to dive into is process optimization. Think of this as decluttering your business processes. Make them sleek and efficient. If it's manufacturing products, we look at it like a manufacturing line. By automating repetitive tasks, production will speed up, errors will go down, and quality will go up. It's about doing more with less, doing it smarter. We've all heard the saying, work smarter, not harder. Not only did I serve as the chief operating officer for years in the corporate world before launching my own businesses, but I also served as VP of operations, and I traveled around teaching other businesses how to optimize their operational structure.

Another thing that we covered when I went into these businesses was process optimization. We want to streamline all our processes to eliminate inefficiencies and especially redundancies. The more you can reduce the time or money spent on something, the more profits. That might be more time back for you to utilize to grow in sales or reduced labor costs. Streamlining your processes will also help you produce better quality.

I would ask them to map each of their processes. If the company did not already have a standard operating procedure (SOP), we wanted to create that for them so that we could map out each process. We must know all the processes and what they do. Visualize each process step on a flowchart to identify bottlenecks. Are there any roadblocks? Is there anything that's jamming things up? We want to remove whatever's holding up the traffic so it can flow down the road. That's what you want to do with your business. Are there any repetitive tasks you can automate? You can use tools like Zapier and Asana to automate routine tasks. Conduct regular reviews and schedule periodic reviews of your processes to find improvement areas. Store all your SOPs in one location so you can quickly review them. This also helps when you bring on new team members as you expand. It provides consistency, continuity, and a level of quality. This is another area where consistency is essential. That allows us to find the right process quickly, map it out, automate anything we can, and review it regularly to ensure it is optimized.

The next thing I teach businesses when I come in is leveraging technology. Leveraging and using modern technology to enhance and streamline operations will save you time and money and make you efficient on the back end. Some tips around this for beginners. Stay updated. Keep abreast of the latest technological trends that apply to your industry. That might mean you need to outsource some of that as you grow. It doesn't have to be WOOS IT or Next Level Connected. But you want to put it with somebody who keeps abreast of these updates in IT. They're learning it daily, seeing the new technologies emerge, and they're part of building the latest technologies that emerge. We're looking for innovative technology that solves problems and gaps for our clients. Look at outsourcing to a specialist if you don't feel that you're going to be best at staying on top of the latest trends in technology. Make sure that you invest wisely. Focus on technologies that solve problems or improve efficiency within your processes. It is so easy to get overwhelmed and distracted, even with technology. Ensure you're taking advantage of what you can and optimizing your resources. Part of this will be employee training. Ensure that your team is trained and comfortable with the new technologies so you can invest wisely and understand what will solve their problems and efficiency slowdowns. If you need help, you can outsource this and bring in a full-time in-house person, but that will cost you more.

Fostering a Culture of Innovation

Encouraging creativity and new ideas is essential for innovation. I teach businesses to allow experimentation—letting team members spend a small percentage of their time on projects related to the business. For example, if someone wants to explore a new technology that could save 20% of your budget by automating processes, let them. Acknowledge and validate their ideas, even if you don't use them immediately. This makes team members feel a part of the vision and encourages continuous input. Create an environment where ideas are freely shared without fear of rejection. Even if the idea isn't fully implemented, listen, and use the feedback. You don't need to allocate massive resources—start small, even 5%, and encourage a creative, problem-solving mindset.

Data-Driven Decision-Making

Data is your GPS—it guides you where you need to go. But like any GPS, it may not always show you the obstacles ahead, such as accidents or roadblocks. That's where your intuition comes in. While data should drive 85% of decisions, the remaining 15% relies on intuition built from experience. If something feels off, listen to that instinct. Use data analysis tools like Google Analytics or Tableau and invest in team training to improve data literacy. Always test and learn—use A/B testing to make informed adjustments based on your data, but don't ignore gut feelings when making critical decisions.

Customer-Centric Operations

Designing operations around customer needs and satisfaction is key. Often, businesses get lost in optimizing processes and forget about the customer. Know your customers' pain points and challenges before they arise and address them. Collect and analyze customer feedback regularly to keep your finger on the pulse of what they need. Personalize the experience using data and customer journey mapping. In my previous roles, we worked heavily on understanding the customer journey, especially in call centers, and making data-driven decisions to improve their experience. Customer-focused operations ensure your business not only runs efficiently but also stays attuned to what really matters—your customers.

Continuous Improvement

Continuous improvement is crucial in every aspect of your business. Regularly assess and improve your operations, starting with small, incremental changes. Analyze SOPs, processes, and feedback to spot inefficiencies and adjust. Listen to your team—those on the ground often see the bottlenecks and pain points firsthand. Having a true open-door policy, not just one written on the wall, allows team members to suggest meaningful improvements. Their input can be a powerful tool in optimizing processes that best serve your customers and organization. Conduct regular audits to identify areas for improvement and ensure team suggestions are incorporated.

Resource Allocation

As your business scales, strategic resource allocation is essential. Focus on areas with the highest return on investment (ROI), regularly reassessing your budget to shift resources from low-performing areas to those that drive real profitability. It's about maximizing profit margins, not just chasing revenue. For instance, a company making $500,000 with a $150,000 spend is more profitable than one making $1 million while spending $900,000. When I work with businesses, the goal is always to push them to the next level—while ensuring that growth results in genuine profitability. That's why I go by *The Profitability Pathmaker* on social media.

Scalability is just as crucial. I often step in when a business grows fast but is unprepared operationally. They may have started with processes that didn't evolve with them, leading to chaos and inefficiency as they scaled. Without a foundation for scalability, rapid growth can harm your brand, and in some cases, even put you out of business. Next Level Connected gets calls because businesses suddenly find themselves in this situation—they're making more money but struggling with poor quality, high turnover, and profit losses. These issues arise because they didn't build with a scalable mindset. The solution? Design a business model that grows with you, not one that holds you back. Investing in scalable infrastructure is essential. While it may cost a little more monthly, it allows for seamless expansion as you add new team members and clients, preventing bottlenecks. Many businesses need the Profitability Pathmaker when their quality drops, team members leave, and they're losing money despite making more than ever. This happens because they weren't built to scale. A scalable infrastructure ensures that your business can grow without sacrificing quality or profitability. Ask yourself, "How can I scale this? Will this work as I expand?" Always build with the future in mind.

Consider hiring a business coach or strategist who can foresee growth challenges and address them proactively. Scalable systems are adaptable, enabling your processes to flex as you grow. Regularly forecast growth—not just budget, sales, and recruitment. I've seen businesses close or experience chaotic growth due to inflexible processes and a lack of preparation. Your business needs the ability to expand without breaking under the pressure of rapid growth. This foundation of operational efficiency on the back end of your business will allow you to scale profitably. In the upcoming sections, we'll explore core principles and practical steps for implementing scalable, profitable systems that take your business beyond the seven or eight-figure mark.

Amplifying Business Growth through Systems

We're going to be talking about amplifying business growth through systems. Last time, we touched on some core principles for understanding operational efficiency. We'll review the basics quickly. Operational efficiency is like a business' magic wand. It's about doing things the smart way, not the hard way, optimizing your processes, and ensuring that every dollar, minute, and resource counts. It's about working smarter, not harder. Why does it matter? Operational efficiency is going to be the lifeblood of your back end. When you have efficient operations in your business, you'll be saving money. You're going to be reducing waste and increasing your profit margins. We talked a bit about the difference between generating gross revenue and your actual profit margin. To simplify it further, it's the difference between thriving and surviving in the business world. When your operations are humming along smoothly, you're not only reducing your costs, but also using your resources wisely. This will mean more money in your pocket and higher profit margins. We want to take our business past the seven or eight-figure mark. That's our goal. But our goal is to yield a significant profit margin. You want a profitable business. Operational efficiency will be a critical puzzle piece for profitability and taking your business past that seven, eight-figure mark. We touched a little on amplifying business growth through systems and the fact that systems are the backbone of scaling a business. Systems provide structure and consistency, enabling businesses to grow without losing control over their operations.

Email Marketing

Email marketing is one of the easiest places to implement automation. With tools like MailChimp and HubSpot, even non-tech-savvy users can set up workflows to automate personalized campaigns. Most platforms now have built-in or user-friendly automation features, making it simple to segment your audience and tailor messages accordingly. If you're unsure which tool to choose, consider factors like your email list size, budget, ease of use, and the features you need. Remember, you don't need to pay for features you won't use. Look for platforms that scale as your business grows, offering tiered pricing that fits your current and future needs. When segmenting your list, consider customer behavior, demographics, or even psychographics. For example, if you're selling supplements, you might segment by previous purchase behavior, gender-specific products, or even age groups. This ensures the right message reaches the right audience. You could send targeted campaigns to customers who haven't purchased in six months, those on a subscription plan, or those who've abandoned their cart.

Email automation can save you hours each week. Set up workflows like cart abandonment emails that send automatically, or re-engagement emails for customers who haven't ordered in a while. Automate follow-ups for subscription cancelations with offers or adjustments to keep them on board. With automated systems, you'll save time while maintaining personalized engagement. Performance tracking tools in these platforms allow you to analyze results and fine-tune your approach, ensuring better outcomes without the manual work.

Inventory Management & CRM Systems

Inventory management software is crucial in various industries. In my restaurants, for example, our software tracks stock levels, connects to our POS system, and automates reordering based on sales patterns. It can even forecast future demand by analyzing previous years' data and current trends. It also tracks food costs, alerting us to price changes and potential savings. Different industries have different needs, so finding inventory software that suits your business—whether it's for restaurants, retail, or services—is key. For service-based businesses like Next Level Connected's IT division, inventory management is still essential. We keep track of equipment like monitors, card readers, and security systems for clients, such as restaurants and law enforcement. Team members can scan items in and out of the warehouse, and the system alerts us when stock runs low, saving time on manual tracking. In the med spa I owned, we used similar software to manage skincare products and medical supplies. Automation helped reduce labor costs and errors while improving quality control. Over time, this saved us significant amounts, particularly in food costs, where even a 10% savings on large weekly orders is substantial.

When selecting inventory management software, look for systems that integrate with your POS and other sales channels. Use decision-making matrices to compare costs, benefits, and features to find the best fit for your business. Automation, like low stock alerts and automatic reordering, can save hours of manual work and reduce errors.

Customer Relationship Management (CRM) systems are just as important for managing client interactions and sales leads. I use tools like Salesforce, HubSpot, Zoho, and Autotask across various divisions. These platforms help automate workflows, generate reports, and manage customer follow-ups. For instance, at the med spa, our CRM automatically generated reports for clients overdue for Botox, allowing us to follow up with offers and reminders. Automated systems like this save time and ensure no customer falls through the cracks.

Distinct CRM Features & Automation Tools

When selecting a CRM, choose one that aligns with your industry, budget, and business needs. Customize your CRM to fit your sales process and automate follow-up emails. Most CRMs offer integrations with other platforms like email services and POS systems, enabling everything to work together efficiently. This saves time and money, even for solopreneurs, as it allows you to focus on growth instead of repetitive tasks.

Another key area for automation is social media management. Tools like Hootsuite, Sprout Social, and Metrical let you schedule posts, monitor engagement, and track performance. You can batch-create content, schedule it for weeks in advance, and track the analytics to see which content resonates with your audience. This saves hours and improves your social media strategy. Accounting and invoicing software can also be automated to manage finances, generate invoices, and track expenses. Popular tools like QuickBooks allow you to automate recurring invoices, saving time on manual entries. If you don't have a finance team, these tools are essential for maintaining cash flow and tracking profitability. Look for systems that integrate with your CRM or POS to streamline processes.

For businesses handling customer support, ticketing systems are invaluable. In our IT division, we use a ticketing system to track requests, manage projects, and assign tasks geographically. This ensures service level agreements are met and automates much of the support process. Whether it's adding new menu items in a restaurant or managing IT requests, ticketing systems enhance efficiency and accountability. Automating these systems saves hours of manual labor, reduces errors, and allows you to focus on strategic growth rather than operational bottlenecks.

Automating Customer Inquiries and Ticketing Systems

Using a ticketing system for customer inquiries, returns, defects, and complaints can streamline your service process. Tools like Freshdesk, Zendesk, Help Scout, or Autotask can categorize, prioritize, and automate responses. These systems ensure faster response times, help meet client expectations, and minimize errors that often occur with manual processes. By automating ticketing, nothing falls through the cracks, increasing customer satisfaction while saving time and money.

Inventory Management & Automation

Automated systems can also reduce human errors in inventory management. For instance, showing up at the warehouse only to find out items were manually miscounted, wastes time and resources. Automation minimizes mistakes, improves efficiency, and boosts customer satisfaction by keeping everything updated and accessible. As you implement these systems, evaluate which tools are best suited for your business to save time and money.

The Power of Streamlined Operations

Streamlining operations is critical for saving time and money by identifying and addressing bottlenecks and inefficiencies. Start by mapping out your key business processes, even if they seem straightforward. Documenting these processes (SOPs) ensures consistency, especially as your business scales or team members change. It might seem tedious, but it's crucial for long-term success.

Involving Your Team

Ask your team for input when mapping out processes. They often know firsthand where bottlenecks occur and may have valuable suggestions for improvement. When issues are identified, brainstorm solutions as a team. Sometimes redistributing tasks or finding the right tool can significantly reduce inefficiencies and prevent frustration or burnout. Ignoring these issues can lead to wasted resources, high attrition rates, and lost talent—problems that could be avoided with better process management.

Retaining Talent and Optimizing Operations

One red flag in any business is difficulty keeping talented team members. Often, team frustration stems from inefficiencies that make jobs harder and less productive. Optimization means using resources efficiently, getting more out of your efforts. Start by examining expenses and operations to identify areas of overspending or opportunities for improvement. For example, when I reviewed my med spa's frequent product orders, I realized we could get a 30% discount by ordering in bulk, significantly boosting profitability. This kind of cost-cutting can make a big difference. Open communication with your team is essential during this process, as they may offer valuable suggestions. Optimize your supply chain for further cost savings, but implement changes gradually to monitor their impact on other processes and team morale. For example, reducing material waste in manufacturing should be phased in to see its effect over time and to ensure it's beneficial.

Customer Satisfaction and Efficiency

Happy customers are loyal customers. It costs more to acquire new customers than to keep existing ones, and efficiency directly impacts customer satisfaction. Review your customer-facing processes—are there delays in inquiries, order processing, or delivery? These inefficiencies may hurt customer loyalty. Implementing a CRM system helps keep track of customer interactions and ensures no one falls through the cracks. Monitor customer feedback before and after implementing any changes to ensure improvements in satisfaction and response times. By tackling bottlenecks and inefficiencies, you'll not only save money but also improve both customer and team satisfaction, setting the stage for business growth into the seven- or eight-figure range.

Supply Chain Management for Success

Let's dive into supply chain management, an area crucial for both product-based and service-based businesses. Even in service-based industries like digital marketing or IT, inventory management is often necessary—whether for client handbooks or hardware.

Just-in-Time Inventory Management

This method ensures you keep only the amount of inventory to meet immediate demand. It's ideal for businesses scaling past seven or eight figures. To implement it, track your essential products, sales, and customer demand patterns to know how much to reorder and when. For example, in my med spa, we automated inventory management to avoid overstocking and product expiration, which led to lost profits. Using tools and systems to manage inventory helps prevent these issues. You'll need to balance just-in-time inventory with bulk orders when discounts make sense and cash flow is sufficient.

Demand Forecasting

Analyze historical sales data and trends to predict future demand. In my restaurant business, we use this data to prepare for seasonal fluctuations, such as knowing that catering spikes in January while IT services slow down early in the year. By understanding your busy and slow seasons, you can optimize your inventory orders, avoid waste, and ensure you're prepared for high-demand periods.

Building Strong Supplier Relationships

Work closely with reliable suppliers and use inventory management software to automate reorders. Start by applying just-in-time management to a few products, then expand it as you gain confidence.

Optimize Stock Levels

Maintaining the right balance between having enough stock to meet demand and avoiding overstock is crucial. Continuously monitor stock levels, adjust orders based on sales data, and use forecasting tools to optimize inventory. This helps reduce carrying costs and improves cash flow, contributing to overall business health.

Cutting Overhead Costs

Non-essential overhead can quickly add up. Regularly review expenses like software subscriptions or office supplies to identify unnecessary costs. In one case, a client unknowingly paid thousands in unused subscriptions. Categorize your expenses into essentials (rent, utilities) and non-essentials, then involve your team in finding areas to reduce costs without affecting productivity. Use cost management software to track and reduce overhead, freeing up funds for strategic investments and increasing profitability.

Some Strategies for Reducing Your Overhead

Once you've identified the non-essential overhead, it will be time to implement some cost-cutting strategies. Negotiate with your suppliers. That's the first one I always throw out to clients. Negotiate better deals with your suppliers. You can look at bulk purchases to get a discount. You can sometimes do extended payment terms, a 90-day net. The great thing is you can often ask, and there might be something that will work. I cannot tell you how frequently somebody said, "Oh, no, that is the cost." We called and found out that it wasn't just the cost. Guess what? They could save another 10% just by asking. It can't hurt to ask.

Second, if your organization supports remote or hybrid work options, you can look at it. Consider allowing team members to work remotely to reduce office space and related costs. That saves on your utilities. You might do a hybrid model where you're in two days a week and home for three. I have a client that does a lot of different production and video, and they implement a three-day in-office work week. They're all there Monday, Wednesday, and Friday, and nobody's in the office Tuesday or Thursday. They sublease that section of space out to an insurance broker that brings clients on Tuesdays and Thursdays. It works out, and they're able to save **money** on their overall lease. It reduces some costs within their employee base. Look to see if that's an option for you. Implement energy-saving measures in your workplace to lower your utility bills. Make sure the water's not running in the break room sink. Make sure that the lights are turned off. I can't tell you how often I go in, and I'm like, why is this light on? I always go by and shut it off. If nobody's in there, shut the light off. If you implement these strategies one at a time and track their impact on your overhead costs, you'll see little bits add up more and more, making you more profitable.

You should regularly review cost-cutting strategies. We said this in an earlier chapter, but ensure they remain effective, and you can't improve upon them. Suppose you can control inventory management, demand forecasting, and cost reduction strategies. In that case, you will not entirely enhance your supply chain but save a lot of money. Guess what that does? It sets the stage for scaling your business past seven or eight figures. Keep that in mind.

Process Optimization

To optimize your business processes, start with streamlining workflows. Begin by mapping out each workflow step-by-step and identifying bottlenecks. This is where Standard Operating Procedures (SOPs) are essential—they ensure consistency, quality, and preparedness for scaling or unexpected staff changes. From my experience, I've seen how the absence of documented processes can slow growth. For example, when a key leader left without SOPs, it took significant time and effort to rebuild, which set the company back. Avoid this by creating clear SOPs for every core process in your business.

Here's how to approach it:

Map Processes: Visualize each step using tools like flowcharts or whiteboards. Involve your team—they know the day-to-day details and can offer insights into where bottlenecks occur.

Identify Bottlenecks and Wastes: Lean Principles help by highlighting waste like overproduction and excess inventory. Simplify your processes by eliminating redundancies.

Encourage Continuous Improvement: Foster a culture where team members are encouraged to spot inefficiencies and suggest solutions. Recognize their input—it's crucial for building a culture of innovation.

Christy's Key Takeaway: Avoid the "we've always done it that way" trap. Embrace a growth mindset, where inefficiencies are opportunities for improvement. Use lean management tools and project management software to visualize and track tasks, ensuring that processes are efficient. Before a company-wide rollout, test any process changes on a small scale, gather feedback, and refine. Small businesses can start by targeting digital marketing strategies for high ROI and expanding from there.

Additional Marketing Strategies and Resource Allocation

You don't have to implement everything at once. Instead, refine processes gradually and assess their impact on operations. Don't hesitate to seek help. If you can't afford business coaching, leverage networking as a free resource. Many experienced professionals will share insights that can be as effective as paid coaching. Always evaluate how advice applies to your specific business.

Resource Allocation Strategies

Efficient resource allocation is essential. Make the most of what you have by prioritizing your goals and aligning your resources with your business's current and future objectives. Regularly reassess and refine your resource allocation to ensure scalability. Resource management software can help track and optimize your use of resources.

Balancing Workload and Workforce is key for both efficiency and employee satisfaction. A satisfied team builds a strong business. If you're a solopreneur, consider outsourcing or using virtual assistants to fill gaps and reduce workloads. Flexible staffing options, such as part-time or fractional virtual assistance, can help manage busy periods without the cost of full-time hires. Continuously monitor workload balance to prevent burnout and promote productivity.

Workforce management tools can help you track and schedule employee workloads, ensuring optimal productivity. Encouraging a goal-oriented mindset helps employees feel accomplished, boosting morale and performance. Consider different resource allocation models (ROI-based, priority-based, or need-based) to customize strategies that align with your business goals. The key is to evaluate whether your current setup is scalable. Ask yourself: will this help me reach the next level? Aim for long-term growth, and keep scalability in mind.

Christie's Key Takeaway

You don't need to do it all alone. Leverage technology, optimize resources, and seek external help when necessary. Focus on scaling efficiently and paving the way to long-term success, reaching beyond seven and eight figures. Stay persistent, keep learning, and trust the process—you're on the right path to success.

Embracing Technology for Efficiency

To reach seven or eight figures, leveraging automation is a must. Think of automation as your virtual assistant for repetitive tasks. Identify tasks you regularly handle, like email outreach or data entry, and find tools to automate them. For example, email marketing automation can handle everything from follow-up sequences to newsletters, letting you focus on delivering valuable content. By automating tasks like order confirmations or social media posts, you'll free up hours each week and boost efficiency. Monitor your automation's effectiveness by tracking metrics like open rates and accuracy. For customer interactions, consider chatbots for routine inquiries. If you're not sure where to start, consider hiring a business coach or strategist. The key is to continuously refine these automated processes for the best return on investment (ROI).

Next up is data-driven decision-making. The more data you gather, the better you can tailor your business strategies. Tools like Google

Analytics or Excel offer valuable insights, even if you start small. If you're managing customer feedback and sales data, integrating these into a single dashboard can streamline your responses and improve decision-making. Using Business Intelligence (BI) Tools takes data analysis to the next level. These tools offer features like dashboards and predictive analytics, helping you foresee market trends and make proactive decisions. Ensure any BI tool you choose is scalable, so it can grow with your business. This will allow you to integrate data from multiple sources like sales, finance, and marketing for a complete picture of your business performance.

Decision-Making through Data Insights is essential. Schedule regular reviews of data with your team, or if it's just you, dedicate time on your calendar to assess the numbers. Running what-if scenarios with your data can help you anticipate challenges and make contingency plans. Remember: data is your GPS, guiding you where to go. Let it lead 85-90% of your decision-making, with intuition providing the final touch. Building a data-driven culture helps ensure that choices are based on solid insights rather than just gut feelings. The intuition that you rely on will always be there as your experience builds, but data should be your primary guide. By embracing automation and a data-focused approach, you're setting up not just for rapid growth but for smart, sustainable success. Next, we'll dive into Lean Six Sigma principles to streamline even further. Until then, start implementing these tips and watch your business transform.

Making Complex Concepts Simple

In this section, we'll break down resource allocation models and some basic Lean Six Sigma principles to help streamline your business operations and scale toward seven or eight figures.

Resource Allocation Models are frameworks for efficiently distributing resources. Here's how to simplify them:

Understand the Basics: Learn the principles of ROI-based, priority-based, or need-based models. Analyze case studies of businesses using these models effectively and consider how they align with your business goals. Remember, there isn't a one-size-fits-all approach—you may need to combine models that suit your specific needs.

Customize for Your Business: Choose a resource allocation model based on your business's current and future goals. Study successful examples in your industry and run small-scale trials to practice implementing the model. Adapt as necessary, and always seek expert advice if needed.

Flexibility is Key: Your goals and needs may shift, so keep evaluating and refining the model you choose.

Lean Six Sigma focuses on process improvement through reducing waste and increasing efficiency. You don't need formal certification to apply the basic principles:

Start Simple: Familiarize yourself with the core Lean Six Sigma principles—reducing waste and improving efficiency. Watch YouTube tutorials, attend webinars, or use free resources to get an overview.

Data-Driven Problem Solving: Lean Six Sigma revolves around a structured approach: define, measure, analyze, improve, and control. Use this framework to streamline processes and achieve high levels of quality and efficiency in your operations.

Lean Tools: Incorporate tools like value stream mapping (which helps visualize processes and identify inefficiencies) and the 5S method (sort, set in order, shine, standardize, sustain). These tools help improve workflow, minimize waste, and keep processes organized.

Apply Lean Six Sigma Gradually:

- Start with small pilot projects to test these concepts.
- Train your team and encourage them to suggest improvements.
- Keep focusing on continuous improvement and integrating these principles into various departments.

Key Takeaway: Always challenge the status quo. When you hear phrases like "We've always done it that way," it's time to rethink your approach. Encourage innovation and process improvement. Small, continuous steps toward efficiency will set you up for scalability.

Conclusion

We've covered a lot—delving into operational efficiency and innovation to give you strategies that can transform your business. But learning is only step one. The true power lies in applying these insights to your own world. With the foundational tools we've explored, you're ready to streamline operations and foster a culture of innovation. Picture your business running like a well-tuned engine, with every part working in harmony toward unmatched success. Now, you're equipped to make efficiency and innovation the heartbeat of your growth.

As we move forward, get ready to explore the soul of your business: leadership and team building. This next chapter is all about inspiring, motivating, and leading teams that don't just meet targets—they surpass them. I've worked with teams and leaders nationwide, helping them unlock their potential, from small businesses to large state agencies. Now, I'm bringing that experience to you. We'll dive into building a culture where each team member feels valued, heard, and inspired to bring their best. You'll learn the secrets to becoming not just a leader, but the leader that others aspire to follow.

Are you ready to build a team that thrives, excels, and wins together? If so, let's embark on this journey into leadership and team building. Together, we'll create teams that don't just show up—they thrive, grow, and lead themselves. Your transformation into an extraordinary leader starts here, and I can't wait to be part of it.

Chapter 9 Leadership and Team Building

This chapter is one of my favorites because it's not just about creating leaders or building teams—it's about inspiring greatness. If you're starting your business or leading a team, this is your opportunity to shape your workplace culture and ensure it drives your business toward seven or eight figures. Leadership isn't just a possibility—it's a certainty, and it's the force that will propel your business forward.

Lead with Purpose and Passion

Leadership is about guiding your team through uncharted waters. It's about making decisions that inspire trust and confidence. Team building is the glue that turns a group of individuals into an unstoppable force. Both leadership and team building are powerful tools within your reach. You're not just learning to be a leader—you're practicing the skills needed to inspire and motivate your team. When you have a team aligned with a single vision, mission, and goal, you're setting the stage for success.

Awaken Your Inner Leader

Leadership is not just about guiding, but about inspiring your team. We're going to discuss strategies that have worked for me, my businesses, and extraordinary leaders I've known. These are real-world strategies that you can apply to your business. It's crucial to remember that our job as leaders is not just to manage, but to inspire, motivate, and support our teams. When you build and empower your team, they, in turn, build your business. This is the key to moving past seven figures and reaching eight figures and beyond.

By sharing the wisdom I've gained from my experiences and the insights of the incredible mentors I've had, we'll explore how to become truly inspirational leaders. Your role is to provide that inspiration and motivation to your team, and when they feel supported, they will drive your business to new heights.

Foundations of Leadership

Let's dive into the foundations of leadership. I've had the privilege of traveling across the U.S. to train corporations, leaders, and agencies on building solid leadership foundations, and I'm excited to share that knowledge with you. While it's easy to overlook leadership when scaling your business to seven or eight figures, it's one of the most critical components for sustainable growth.

Remember this rule: You build a great team, and your team builds your business.

High turnover, a stressful environment, and workplace toxicity will make it hard to retain talented team members—and that turnover costs you money. Each time someone leaves, you're investing in recruiting and training someone new. That's why leadership is key to creating an environment where people want to be part of a unified vision and mission.

Leadership is the Key to Business Success

Leadership is about continuously developing yourself and evolving your skills. While you may have strong leadership abilities now, there's always room to grow. Leadership is not something you *master* and set aside; it's a skill that should evolve alongside your team's needs.

True leadership revolves around people. If you can read people, understand what they want, and help solve their problems, you will succeed. Business is all about people—whether it's your team, your customers, or your network. So, if we want to grow our business, we must embrace this idea: our business is people. The more we empower, support, and uplift our team and clients, the more success we'll see.

Understanding Leadership Styles

Scaling your business isn't just about growth; it's about guiding your team toward a shared vision. Leadership goes beyond managing—it's about inspiring and empowering others to reach their full potential. Effective leaders not only communicate the company's goals but also energize their teams to act.

I believe in authentic leadership. This means being genuine, transparent, and leading with integrity. People know when leadership is real or just for show. Giving a powerful speech is one thing, but living those words daily is what truly inspires. If you want your team to believe in the vision, you need to embody those values consistently. Lead by Example: If you expect high performance, model it yourself. If you promote an open-door policy, make sure you're truly available to your team when they need support. Integrity is key—it means following through on promises and always doing what's right for your team, clients, and vendors alike. Authentic leaders also embrace vulnerability. Sharing your own struggles doesn't make you weak; it makes you relatable. By opening up, you create deeper connections and build trust. Your team sees you as not just a leader, but as someone real and human, which strengthens your bond with them.

Building Trust and Meaningful Relationships

Once you've built trust and formed meaningful relationships within your team, you'll start seeing the positive effects on your workplace culture. People want to be part of something they believe in. When your leadership fosters a positive, motivating environment, it becomes magnetic—it draws in talent and retains it. Just like charisma and confidence are practiced skills, leadership is something you develop through demonstrated behaviors.

Key Traits of Influential Leaders

To scale your business, you need to guide a team toward a shared vision. Leadership is more than management; it's about inspiring and empowering others to achieve their potential. Here's what sets influential leaders apart:

Vision: Effective leaders have a clear vision and communicate it well. Without clarity, teams can't follow effectively. A clear vision keeps everyone aligned and focused.

Inspiration: Great leaders motivate their teams to buy into the vision and contribute to the business's success.

Integrity: True leaders live their values. They lead by example and make the right decisions, even when they're tough.

Vulnerability: Being open and honest builds trust. Leaders who show vulnerability are relatable and foster deeper connections within the team.

Successful leadership is the bedrock of business growth. Prioritizing people—empowering and supporting them—sets the foundation for success.

Empathy: Empathy doesn't mean you agree with everything; it means you understand and care about your team members' needs. This connection helps you design plans that support their success and create a positive business environment.

Communication: Exceptional leaders are clear communicators. It's not about being the most eloquent; it's about conveying ideas and vision effectively.

Decisiveness: Leaders make countless decisions daily. Quick, informed decisions, grounded 85% in data and 15% in intuition, drive effective leadership.

Adaptability: Embrace change and be open to pivoting. Listen to diverse perspectives, then align them under one mission and goal.

Resilience: Stay positive and resilient, especially in challenging times. Setbacks are part of the journey, but bouncing back and maintaining calm will inspire your team to do the same.

Leadership Styles: Finding Your Approach

Transformational Leadership: These leaders inspire innovation by creating a shared vision and fostering growth.

Servant Leadership: Leaders who prioritize their team's well-being often cultivate loyalty and commitment. The mindset is to serve others first.

Visionary Leadership: Visionaries offer a compelling future vision, inspiring teams to work toward it.

You don't have to fit into one style. Combine approaches in a way that aligns with your personality and values. While it's crucial to stay authentic, blending different leadership styles can enhance your impact.

Consistency in values is essential. Leadership is about staying true to your core values, regardless of external pressures. Authenticity is key, but evolving and embracing new ideas can help you become a well-rounded leader. Remember, your values are your foundation, but your leadership style can adapt to bring out the best in others.

Learn from Other Leaders

Study other successful leaders, and you'll gain valuable insights into different leadership mindsets and strategies. Observing how others craft their vision and inspire their teams can give you fresh ideas for your own approach. Look for leaders who:

- Inspire creativity and innovation within their teams.
- Embody servant leadership, dedicating their lives to serving others and leading movements within their communities.

Some leaders blend multiple styles, while others focus on specific aspects of leadership. The key is to absorb what resonates with you and aligns with your core values. Don't mimic someone else's style; instead, take elements from the leaders who inspire you and adapt them to fit your natural approach.

Leadership is Personal

Effective leadership is not a one-size-fits-all concept. It's about finding your unique path and developing your own style while staying true to your values. Authenticity builds trust with your team, and trust inspires them to follow you. When your team sees that you're genuine, consistent, and aligned with your core principles, they're more likely to rally behind your vision. As you grow as a leader, remember that the goal is not only to achieve greatness for yourself, but to inspire greatness in others. When you focus on uplifting your team and empowering them to reach their full potential, you will naturally see success in your business. The first step in building a successful business is to focus on your team members. Ask yourself: How can I elevate them? How can I help them reach their potential? Because ultimately, your team is what will take your business to the next level.

As a leader, embrace your potential by leading with authenticity, purpose, and passion. Remember, you don't have to communicate the same way I do. Your style doesn't need to be as energetic—it just needs to be genuine to you. What matters is that you project positivity, energy, and a clear vision that your team can rally behind.

Leading by Example

Leadership isn't just about creating a mission statement; it's about embodying that mission every day. When your team sees you living the principles you talk about, it creates a workplace culture people want to be a part of. That's how you build an environment where everyone is inspired to contribute. I'm often asked, "How can I change my workplace culture? How do I inspire a team that doesn't seem inspired?" Here's the thing: Everyone is driven by something. It's your role as a leader to find that spark and ignite the passion in your team members. Leadership is about developing others, and that's not always easy.

The Loneliness of Leadership

Leadership can often feel like a lonely path. Why? Because as a leader, you shoulder all the responsibility, take all the risk, and bear all the blame. Meanwhile, you push your team into the spotlight, letting them shine. You may have seen those images of a ladder where the leader is at the bottom, lifting everyone else up. That's how leadership works—you support your team's climb to success while staying in the background.

It's essential to have mentors, colleagues, and peers to lean on, people you can vent to, brainstorm with, and learn from. While you may be alone in some responsibilities, you don't have to walk the path of leadership alone.

Reflect and Improve

Review your leadership style. What aligns with your personality and core values? Where can you improve? Write down specific areas for growth and actively reflect on them.

Next, we'll dive into building high-performing teams, which are crucial for driving exceptional results in your business.

High Performance Teams

Creating high-performing teams is essential for achieving business goals and reaching new levels of success. A fundamental aspect is team dynamics, which refers to how team members interact, communicate, and collaborate. Effective team dynamics foster positive communication and collaboration, which in turn drives goal achievement. Negative dynamics—such as poor communication and working in silos—can be major roadblocks. A cohesive team culture, built on mutual trust, respect, and shared values, allows members to feel comfortable sharing ideas and constructively challenging one another. It's not just about being polite; it's about working together to fill gaps and leveraging individual strengths to create a unified whole. As leaders, we shape this culture by modeling openness, addressing conflicts promptly, and encouraging constructive feedback.

Key Elements for High-Performance Teams

Positive Team Dynamics: A strong team culture is about more than just friendliness—it's about respectful, constructive challenges that help the team grow.

Clear Communication: Just like in the game of telephone, messages can get muddled. Avoid miscommunication by ensuring clarity at every step.

Conflict Resolution: Address conflicts head-on with empathy, focusing on understanding the root cause and developing productive solutions.

Accountability: Holding each other accountable fosters trust and helps maintain a standard of excellence. It's essential to be respectful while ensuring everyone upholds their responsibilities.

Adaptability: Resistance to change stifles growth. Encourage a mindset open to new ideas and changes, reinforcing transparent communication and aligning everyone toward shared goals.

Common Team Challenges and Solutions

Communication Breakdowns: These can lead to confusion and misalignment. Regularly check in with team members and ensure clarity in messaging.

Micromanagement: Continuous feedback is vital, but micromanaging limits a person's ability to work autonomously and hampers innovation. Provide constructive feedback while allowing team members the freedom to navigate their responsibilities.

Resistance to Change: Foster an environment that welcomes new ideas and encourages flexibility. This helps the team stay agile and ready for growth.

Lack of Accountability: Set clear roles and responsibilities. Ensuring each team member knows their role promotes ownership and commitment to achieving the team's goals.

By establishing an environment of open communication and mutual respect, your team will feel empowered to contribute, adapt, and excel. Continuous feedback and encouragement will create a workplace where individuals can thrive autonomously and know when to adjust their course. Building high-performance teams means promoting a culture that values growth, adaptability, and accountability, setting a foundation for long-term success.

Building Trust and Collaboration Through Team-Building Activities

Team-building activities are powerful tools for addressing challenges, enhancing understanding, and fostering trust among team members. When people connect and relate to one another, they are naturally more likely to form trusting bonds. Trust is essential because people work better with those they trust. By focusing on activities that build trust and collaboration, you'll create a more cohesive, efficient, and motivated team. One of the best ways to enhance team cohesion is through fun and engaging team-building exercises. These activities can range from trust-building exercises to problem-solving challenges. For instance, my IT division loves Escape Room challenges. These activities require everyone to work together, using each person's unique strengths to solve puzzles and riddles within a limited timeframe. Escape Rooms are a great way to build teamwork, enhance creativity, and hone critical thinking skills, all of which are crucial for tackling challenges in the workplace.

Workshops and Real-World Problem Solving

Another effective team-building method is to organize workshops with guest speakers or leaders within your organization. These workshops can focus on topics like communication, conflict resolution, and leadership development. I often speak at such workshops, guiding teams through real-life challenges they've faced and using solution-based problem-solving methods to work through them together. These exercises help team members share perspectives and develop valuable skills they may not have considered before.

The Role of Trust in High-Performing Teams

Trust is the foundation of any high-performing team. As a leader, it's your job to foster an environment where team members trust each other's intentions and capabilities. This distinction is key when discussing micromanagement versus frequent feedback. Micromanagement implies a lack of trust. While frequent, constructive feedback builds trust by showing that you believe in your team's abilities and want to support their growth.

Surround yourself with people who are brighter, smarter, and more creative than you. As a leader, you may set the vision, but the execution relies on your team's skills, strengths, and innovation. My job is to support, inspire, and empower my team to reach our collective goals. I want my team members to know I trust them implicitly and that trust isn't diminished if they hit a roadblock and come to me for help.

Open Communication and Vulnerability

Encourage an environment where open communication is the norm. Your team should feel comfortable coming to you with their struggles or challenges without the fear of disappointing you. Let them know it's okay to be vulnerable and that asking for support doesn't diminish your trust in their capabilities. This open-door policy must work both ways. Your team needs to trust that you are approachable, and they need to know that asking for help will not lower their confidence in your eyes. Confidence is crucial for achieving better results. Whether speaking on stage or executing tasks in the workplace, confidence fuels performance. Your job as a leader is to build that confidence through trust, open communication, and constant support.

Creating a High-Performing Team Environment

To build a high-performing team, ensure that each member feels confident in their capabilities and trusts that they can approach you when needed. Foster open and honest communication, where everyone can share thoughts, concerns, and feelings without fear of judgment. By creating this kind of supportive environment, you'll build a team that is not only high-performing but also deeply committed to your shared goals.

Here's a refined version of the section on accountability and team dynamics, with a focus on clarity, practical advice, and inspirational guidance:

The Importance of Accountability in High-Performance Teams

Accountability is a cornerstone of building a high-performance team. It ensures that every team member takes ownership of their tasks and responsibilities. As leaders, it's crucial to set clear expectations and provide regular feedback, so each person knows exactly what's expected of them and how they're performing. Recognizing and rewarding accountability is equally important. Celebrate small wins and achievements to help your team feel fulfilled and empowered. When people feel valued for their contributions, it creates a positive cycle of motivation and engagement.

Adjusting When Things Don't Go as Planned

No team or leader is perfect 100% of the time, and that's okay. It's not about avoiding mistakes, but about how you come back from them. If something doesn't go as planned, ask yourself and your team: What can we learn from this? How can we adjust going forward? Just as in every other area of business, we must continuously seek opportunities for growth and improvement.

Leaders often come to me at conferences, saying, "Christy, our workplace culture might be beyond repair," or "It's so hard to fix things now that we have a bad culture here." While it's true that establishing a positive culture from the beginning is easier, it's never too late to turn things around. No workplace is perfect all the time, but what matters is how you handle those imperfections. Learning from challenges and adjusting strategies is key to long-term success.

Creating a Culture of Vulnerability and Growth

Encourage your team to be vulnerable. When team members will share their struggles, mistakes, and challenges, it creates a supportive environment where growth can happen. As a leader, your role is to motivate, support, and lift up your team. Remember, leadership is about pushing your team up the ladder, not climbing it yourself. There are no shortcuts to building a positive workplace culture. While some companies like Google or Amazon may showcase excellent team dynamics, their strategies can be adapted and applied on a smaller scale to your business. Learn from them, but don't feel you need to replicate their methods exactly. Instead, focus on what works for your team and your unique situation.

Commitment to Continuous Improvement

Building a high-performance team is an ongoing process that requires continuous effort. Even when something works well, there's always room to refine and improve. Ultimately, success in leadership comes down to commitment—commitment to your team members, to growth, and to shifting your mindset to focus on helping others succeed. When you focus on the people around you, they will guide your business in the right direction. Whether you're leading a large team or just starting out as a solopreneur, think about the dynamics you want to build with your future team members. Consider how you'll foster positive relationships and effective team dynamics as your business grows.

Looking Ahead: Visionary Leadership and Growth

In the next session, we'll explore the leader's role in growth and visionary leadership. I'm excited to dive into how you can help others reach their full potential while continuing to grow yourself. Empowering and uplifting others is at the heart of great leadership, and I look forward to sharing more ways you can inspire your team and steer your business to success.

The Leader's Role in Growth

As a leader, you're responsible for setting a compelling vision that drives your business forward. A visionary leader not only has a clear view of the company's future but also knows how to inspire others to embrace it. Begin by reflecting on your core values and business purpose. Define what you want to achieve, your goals, and how you aim to impact your industry and community. Your vision should be ambitious yet attainable, resonating with your team's values and aspirations. Once you've defined this vision, the next step is communication. Share it passionately and consistently—use storytelling and vivid language to make it come alive. People are drawn to leaders who convey excitement and belief in their vision, so make sure your enthusiasm is evident. Paint a vivid picture of the future, and actively involve your team in it. Show them how their individual roles contribute to this shared vision. Don't wait for an annual meeting to inspire your team; keep the conversation going. Let them feel that they're integral to this journey. They're not just employees; they're essential contributors to your company's future success. Engage your team emotionally, make them feel connected, and ensure they see how their efforts directly tie into achieving something meaningful. A consistently communicated vision will keep your team motivated, aligned, and invested in reaching the next level of growth together.

Empowering Every Role to Contribute to the Vision

One of the most crucial aspects of leadership is ensuring that every team member understands how their role contributes to the overall vision of the company. It doesn't matter what the position is—everyone plays a part in the business's success. This is especially important when fostering a positive culture and driving a team toward a shared goal. For example, I had a young lady working as a cashier at one of my Atlanta Bread Company locations in Woodstock. She came to me and said, "Christy, *I'm just* in high school. I know I'm just cashiering, so I don't have a big part in this restaurant's future." I quickly corrected her, explaining how critical her role is. She is on the front lines interacting with customers, and without those customer interactions, we wouldn't have a business. We discussed how her role is directly connected to the growth of the brand and explored the ways she could become more involved in shaping that vision. By showing her how important her position was, she left feeling more inspired and empowered to contribute meaningfully.

Debunking the *Just a*...Myth

When team members say, "I'm *just a* [insert role]," it's our job as leaders to debunk that myth. There's no such thing as *just a* role—every position is a vital part of the team's success. You need to communicate how each role contributes to the shared vision and align your team with the company's purpose. Encourage open dialogue and ongoing discussions about the company's vision. Ask for their input on how they feel they are shaping the path forward. When everyone understands their importance, they're more likely to feel motivated and committed to achieving the company's goals.

Creating Clear Goals and Action Plans

To foster a sense of ownership, break down the big picture into smaller, actionable steps. This helps your team see how their daily tasks are moving the business forward. Concrete goals and action plans allow everyone to feel like they are actively contributing to the larger vision.

For many organizations, performance reviews often cause stress, especially when they only happen once a year. In the months leading up to the review, people scramble to meet goals. This is why I prefer consistent feedback rather than relying solely on annual reviews. At Next Level, even in our restaurants, we provide quarterly sit-downs to review progress. But more importantly, we have daily and weekly check-ins, where managers discuss strengths, growth opportunities, and short-term goals with team members. Frequent conversations about goals—whether short-term or long-term—are crucial for fostering ownership and dedication among your team.

The Power of Visionary Leadership

We hear a lot about iconic leaders like Elon Musk or Oprah Winfrey, and one thing they all have in common is a clear vision. They not only know what they want to achieve, but can also inspire their teams to share that vision. This is the essence of visionary leadership: setting a clear, ambitious direction and inspiring your team to believe in it and work toward it. That's the goal we want to achieve as leaders. We need to communicate the vision clearly, break it down into actionable goals, and inspire everyone to get on board with it.

Navigating Change with Empathy

Change is inevitable in business, but it can be unsettling for team members. As leaders, it's our responsibility to navigate change confidently while providing stability and reassurance. During times of transition, it's important to keep the lines of communication open and be transparent about why changes are happening and the benefits they will bring. Empathy is key. Recognize that change can create uncertainty, but by leading with understanding and honesty, you can help your team adapt and remain committed to the shared vision. If there is a challenge, you want to hear about it because the feet on the ground, the people in it each day, will point out things that you might have missed or overlooked. We want to ensure that we are that stable rock, that support during times of change, and we lead and guide the change. We are there for our team. We understand how tough it is, and here's what we will do to alleviate some discomfort. Or here's the shared vision, even within that change. As leaders, we want to stay adaptable and open to new ideas. Even if we are working through a change, we still want to be open to adjusting as necessary throughout that change. Embrace change as an opportunity for growth and improvement. We want to encourage our team to share concerns, ideas, and things to help them effectively manage that change.

Effective Strategies for Managing Change

In the constantly shifting business landscape, the ability to manage change is essential. Effective change management requires clear strategies that not only guide your team through transitions but also empower them to embrace new directions.

1. Communication: As a leader, clear and consistent communication is your most valuable tool. Explain the reasons for change, the expected impact, and the timeline. If adjustments occur, be transparent about why. Open the floor for questions and concerns, and address them honestly. This approach helps ease transitions and builds trust, making it easier for your team to adapt.

2. Team Involvement: Include team members in the decision-making process. Those on the front lines often hold valuable insights that can shape change in effective ways. By seeking their input, you empower them to take ownership of the change, fostering a sense of participation and commitment across the team.

3. Training and Support: Equip your team with the necessary resources, training, and emotional support to adjust smoothly. Recognize that change can be challenging, and show empathy. Create a safe space where team members feel comfortable voicing concerns and asking for help. This support system is crucial in helping them navigate the transition.

4. Monitor and Adjust: Throughout the change process, gather feedback and monitor progress. Pay attention to what's working and be ready to make adjustments as needed. Effective feedback loops ensure that the change is being implemented smoothly and that your team remains aligned and engaged.

By focusing on communication, involvement, support, and feedback, you can lead your team through change with confidence, ensuring they are both prepared and empowered to adapt.

Learning from Success Stories of Change

Change is not just a challenge—it's an opportunity for growth and innovation. Look at examples in the business world where companies thrived through times of significant change. One example is the restaurant industry during COVID-19. Restaurants had to rethink their entire operations to survive. My restaurants had to shift focus, adapt, and change how we operated to stay afloat. Another powerful example is Netflix, which evolved from a DVD rental service to a global leader in streaming. Their willingness to expect change and adapt led to unprecedented growth. Similarly, companies like IBM transitioned from hardware to software and services, keeping them relevant in a rapidly changing tech landscape. These businesses didn't just survive—they thrived because they embraced change.

Becoming Dynamic: A Key Leadership Skill

In business, change is constant. Dynamic leaders are those who not only anticipate change but are also prepared for it. This is why I train my teams to become dynamic—to expect change daily and embrace it as part of their routine. When you cultivate a mindset of adaptability, it becomes easier to handle challenges as they arise. Change is no longer a shock; it becomes something you are ready for. To help your team become more dynamic, offer training on how to anticipate and manage change. Make it a practice to see change as an opportunity for growth. When your team adopts this mindset, they'll be better equipped to turn challenges into success stories.

Leading Through Change

Visionary leadership includes not only having a clear vision for the future but also having the ability to lead through periods of change. As you apply these strategies to your business, think about how you can adapt and grow while leading your team through uncertainty. These skills are crucial for driving business growth. Remember that change fuels growth, and as a leader, your ability to manage and navigate change will help your team—and your business—thrive. By preparing your team, offering support, and fostering open communication, you'll be able to lead through any change with confidence.

In the next session, we'll dive deeper into empowering your team, because that's what truly drives success.

Empowering Your Team

To break through seven- or eight-figure barriers, you need empowered, high-performing teams. Empowering your team gives them the autonomy to make decisions, fostering engagement, motivation, and innovation. When team members feel trusted, they're more likely to take initiative and contribute their best.

1. Trust and Ownership: Empowerment starts with giving team members responsibility and letting them take ownership of their work. When they feel trusted, they're more accountable and committed, often going above and beyond because they feel valued.

2. Effective Delegation: Delegate based on individual strengths, experience, and interests. Clearly define the project, set expectations, and provide necessary resources. Check in regularly but allow room for autonomy. This builds confidence and reduces the need for micromanagement.

3. Collaboration and Growth: Encourage frequent idea-sharing and value team input. Invest in their growth through training and development opportunities. Showing that you're invested in their future fosters loyalty and builds a capable team ready to tackle new challenges.

4. Flexibility and Work-Life Balance: Offering flexibility in scheduling, especially in roles where it's feasible, increases job satisfaction. Align schedules with team members' availability, which can reduce turnover and improve team dynamics.

5. Building Trust: A culture of trust is essential for effective teamwork. Demonstrate trustworthiness by being honest, transparent, and reliable. Hold regular one-on-ones to listen and understand team members' needs. Open communication and consistency are key to building lasting trust.

6. Team-Building and Communication: Organize activities to strengthen relationships and foster teamwork, whether virtual or in-person. Keep lines of communication open with frequent, informal check-ins, which help you stay in touch with team dynamics and address concerns before they escalate.

By empowering your team, maintaining open dialogue, and cultivating trust, you create a motivated, high-performing group that's ready to drive your business forward. Implement these principles, adapting them to fit your unique team dynamics and goals. Regular interaction, attentive listening, and genuine support will foster an environment where team members thrive and contribute their best.

Leading by Example

Authentic leadership is about staying true to your values, leading with integrity, and being genuine—especially during tough times. True leaders inspire trust and loyalty because their actions align with their words. They're not afraid to show vulnerability, which is often seen as a weakness but is, in fact, a strength. Admitting mistakes, seeking help, and sharing challenges build trust and make you more relatable.

1. Embracing Authenticity and Vulnerability: As a leader, it's crucial to be transparent. Share both your successes and failures. These experiences shape who you are and can offer valuable lessons for others. A willingness to be open about your journey fosters deeper connections with your team and demonstrates that learning is a lifelong process.

2. Continuous Improvement: Leadership is an ongoing journey of growth. Regularly seek feedback, learn from mentors, and pursue knowledge through reading, webinars, and networking. This commitment to self-improvement not only strengthens your own skills but also sets a positive example for your team.

3. Fostering a Leadership Culture: Leadership isn't tied to a title—it's about inspiring others. Encourage leadership development at all levels,

and offer training and mentorship opportunities. Empower your team to take on new challenges, make decisions, and grow in their roles. When everyone feels they have a path to grow, they're more engaged and motivated to contribute to the organization's success.

4. Building an Environment of Trust and Empowerment: Trust your team and provide them with the autonomy to excel. Effective delegation allows them to take ownership of their work while you stay available for guidance. Open and honest communication is the foundation for a culture where team members feel secure, valued, and motivated to share their ideas.

As you lead by example and nurture a culture of growth and innovation, you create a workplace where people want to be. Leadership is about lifting others up and fostering a collective drive to achieve shared goals. Next, we'll explore how to scale your business beyond seven figures. Remember, the journey doesn't stop here—true leaders are always looking for ways to grow, innovate, and push beyond the limits.

Chapter 10
On to the Next Level

We've come a long way, but this is where the real work begins—putting everything into action and scaling your business strategically. It's like assembling a puzzle, and now that you have all the pieces, it's time to fit them together and create a bigger, clearer picture of success. Let's talk about scaling beyond seven or eight figures and making your business not only grow but thrive. You've built a foundation, gathered insights, and developed strategies—now it's time to take it further, to aim for sustainable growth that lasts and leaves a legacy. In this phase, we're not just aiming for incremental progress. We're talking about strategic growth that makes your brand a household name, ensuring that what you've built continues to flourish long after you've hit your milestones. This isn't just about dreaming big—it's about turning those dreams into reality through smart, targeted actions.

The Next Steps for Scaling Beyond Seven Figures

We've covered a lot, and now it's time to focus on how you're going to scale. Here's how to put everything into practice:

Recap Financial Literacy: Start by doing a thorough audit of your current financial situation—look at income, expenses, balance sheets, and cash flow. Use tools like QuickBooks or work closely with your accountant to identify areas where you can reduce costs and increase revenue. Understanding your financial foundation is crucial for creating the next steps.

Comprehensive Market Analysis: Know your competition inside and out—what's working for them? Where are their gaps? Just as importantly, deeply understand your target audience—what are their biggest pain points? What keeps them up at night? The more you know, the better you can tailor your products, services, and marketing to perfectly fit their needs.

Gather Customer Feedback: This is all about understanding your customer experience from their point of view. Use surveys, reviews, or even direct conversations to gather insights. The more you know what they think and feel, the better you can fine-tune your offerings to create an exceptional customer journey.

Embrace Innovations: Keep up with trends and industry shifts. That means staying informed about what's happening in your industry and neighboring markets. Follow competitors, industry blogs, and attend webinars or forums. Embracing new technology, automation, and AI-driven analytics is key to staying ahead.

Optimize Operations: If you're not running an efficient business, you're wasting valuable time and money. Review your operational processes and look for areas to streamline. Revisit earlier chapters on improving efficiency and make sure your systems are working for you—not the other way around.

Refine Your Leadership: Whether you're a solopreneur or managing a team, refining your leadership skills is crucial. You need to lead with vision and inspire others to follow that path. But remember, you don't want followers—you want to build leaders within your team. Invest in yourself and in your team's growth through leadership development programs, coaching, and continuous learning.

Now is the time to focus on building a sustainable business that keeps growing. We don't want you just to reach those seven- or eight-figure goals—we want to make sure your business continues thriving. You've built this incredible foundation; now let's scale it smartly.

What happens when we carve out a path and it just ends? No one likes a dead-end job. That's the essence of a dead-end job—feeling like there's nowhere else to go. Make sure you establish a clear career growth path for your team, organization, and clients. Communicate that vision effectively. This is a key part of leadership. Whether you're a leader in your business, industry, or network, work on becoming an inspiring leader. Remember, leadership isn't about being on top. Great leadership pushes everyone up from the foundation. Your job is to empower and uplift from the bottom. Focus on being a better leader daily. Continuously learn, refine, and grow your leadership skills so you can inspire others. The stronger your team, the stronger your business. We don't build businesses alone. We build teams, and those teams build the business. Foster a culture of continuous team-building, training, and development. It's not a onetime event; it's ongoing growth.

Next, ensure you have scalable systems in place. Regularly review business processes for bottlenecks and inefficiencies. Never grow complacent. Invest in scalable technologies that can support future growth. Don't just think about where you are now—think about where you're going. Build an infrastructure that will work when you've grown from five employees to 500 or more. It's more cost-effective to plan for growth now than to rebuild later when it's too late. Embrace a growth mindset and think long-term. Look at expansion and legacy-building. Where do you want your business to go in the next six months? 12 months? Five years? Decide if scaling nationally or globally makes sense for your business. Use market research tools to identify the best opportunities for expansion. As you grow, ensure your brand story and core values resonate with your expanding audience. Our goal isn't just to hit seven or eight figures. It's creating a sustainable business that keeps growing. Once you hit a milestone, you don't stop. You keep pushing. Building a legacy means creating something that will continue producing success for years to come. Make sure your brand identity stays true to your core values but is adaptable enough to resonate with different markets.

How do you put all this into action? Start by creating an action plan. Draft a detailed plan with timelines and clear responsibilities. Translate your strategies into specific tasks with time-bound goals. Break it down—start broad, then focus on individualized steps for each task. Yes, it's a lot of work, but I promise, taking the time to do this will make it easier to reach your goals. I've done this for my businesses—going from zero to seven figures in less than 20 months—and for thousands of clients. The key is not just knowing the strategies, but implementing them. You have the puzzle pieces; now, it's time to put them together and create that big picture.

Review, Adapt, and Stay Flexible

Regularly review your progress and adapt your strategies as needed. Use business analytics and performance tracking tools to stay on top of market changes and your customers' evolving needs. Flexibility and responsiveness are key to staying ahead of your competitors. One of the most critical business skills I've found is training yourself to become dynamic. Expect roadblocks, leverage your weaknesses, and pivot when necessary. Turn challenges into strengths, whether it's learning from them, improving efficiency, or boosting customer satisfaction. If you're small, use that agility to resonate with people in ways that big competitors can't. Train yourself to adapt daily. Create detailed action plans with bite-sized goals and timelines. Be flexible—know that you'll need to modify your plans often as you review them.

Embrace Continuous Learning

Never stop learning. Keep growing through courses, networking, and staying informed. A growth mindset will set you apart from competitors and help you reach the next level. Build a network of peers, mentors, and experts through LinkedIn, forums, and local or virtual events. Make networking a priority—introduce yourself to more people without an agenda. Focus on others—whether customers, team members, or your network. When you shift your focus to helping others, you'll build better relationships, ease anxiety around speaking, and create better products and services.

Focus on Giving

When networking, don't go in with a *sell, sell, sell* mindset. Instead, think *give, give, give.* I promise you'll get more than you give. Stay flexible, embrace a growth mindset, and always look to improve your business. Whether it's reaching seven, eight, or nine figures, always seek ways to refine your products, services, processes, and leadership skills.

Build a Support System

You don't need to do it all alone. Learn from others' failures and successes, and don't be afraid to ask for help. Being vulnerable as a leader is not a weakness. It's essential for growth and success. Surround yourself with a support system and build your network, not only to grow sales but also to grow your team. I don't do everything myself. I rely on my teams and my network. That's how we accomplish so much. During a recent TV interview, someone asked me how I do it all—running multiple businesses, being a speaker, author, mom, wife, and community volunteer. My answer was simple: "I don't." The secret to success is relying on your support system. No one person can do it all.

Create a Sustainable Legacy

Building a support system and network will take your business past seven or eight figures and make it scalable. You're building a legacy that lasts. Whether you choose to sell your business, pass it down, or keep it for yourself, you'll have created something sustainable. This is your year to do it. You've got this.

If you have questions, I'm always here to answer them. If you want to work together professionally and your business needs help, our business, my team, and I are here for you. If you wish to seek help from someone outside of me, I am happy to point you in that direction if that suits you. There are many resources. Some of them are even free. You should take advantage of them. Set clear short-term goals. You want your long-term goals. You're building a sustainable long-term business but wish to define achievable goals, incremental sales improvements, customer satisfaction, and operational efficiency. Use goal-setting templates and apps. Understand that small steps are okay. That's how you achieve your goal.

You will not jump from A to Z overnight. But you aim to go from A to B and then B to C. Take the steps, break it down, and make it attainable and manageable. Like I said, this is your year. Don't be afraid to pivot. Don't be scared to make changes as you're going, and you see what works and what doesn't for your business. Every business is unique. When I enter a company, I do not just hand them a sheet and say, here you go. This is what we're doing. No, I analyze their business and custom-tailor strategies that suit them and will give them the biggest bang for their buck, biggest ROI. Start somewhere. Start with those small steps. That's the key. Start somewhere and build momentum as you go. Remember that scaling a business is a journey. It's not a race. Now that we've come to the end of this journey, the end of *Dollars & Sense-Abilities for Business*

Owners, I hope you feel as empowered and ready to take on the world as I am. We've covered so many tips, strategies, frameworks, and advice.

It's a lot of knowledge floating around. We've talked about mastering your financials and making smart strategic decisions. That is going to drive your business forward. It's understanding the nuts and bolts of business. It isn't just about numbers. It's about creating that path to overall success and stability. We went through the finances. We navigated through decoding people dynamics. How important is that? It's important and so overlooked. We talked about automation and streamlining operational processes. We touched on sales and marketing techniques to dive into. We discussed networking and its importance in scaling a business past seven or eight figures. Here's my challenge to you. I want you to take all these lessons, training, tools, and sensibilities and put them into action. Remember, knowledge is nothing without action.

I want you to take them all and put them into action. Look at your business through a fresh set of glasses and eyes, and see the potential in your numbers and your ability to create something for your team members, clients, and the people in your support network. Embrace the power of informed decision-making. You can steer your business to unimaginable heights. You have that power. You have that knowledge now. You must put it into concrete steps, concrete action. Remember, you're not alone. Reach out, seek advice, and keep learning. The world of business is constantly evolving, and so should we. The world of business is dynamic. It's fast-paced, and it will continuously be changing. That's why we should, too. Let's make a difference in our business. Be bold, be brave, and above all, be wise. Use these strategies wisely.

Let me know. Shoot me an email. Even if we will not work together past this, if nothing else, tell me what worked. Here's my opportunity to solicit feedback. What do you wish I would delve into further? Could I create something for you that would help you understand strategies better? What can I do better? What can I give you? What's working great? I want you to let me know. I want to ride along. I want to hear about the success of your business, and when you've surpassed seven or even eight figures. Thank you for joining me on this empowerment journey, mastering money moves, decoding people dynamics, and soaring past seven or eight figures. Here's to your success!

About the Author

Christy Wilson: Where Strategy Meets Sparkle

Christy Wilson is a seasoned business strategist with nearly 30 years of experience in transforming businesses into multi-million-dollar successes. She's not just another consultant—Christy has built and scaled eight of her own companies and helped countless business owners take their businesses to new levels, with some crossing the eight-figure mark.

In her book, *Dollars & Sense-Abilities for Business Owners*, Christy unveils the real-world strategies and insights that have guided thousands of business owners to long-term success. Her relatable, no-nonsense style brings clarity to even the most complex challenges, empowering readers to break through business barriers and unlock the growth, freedom, and impact they've been working toward.

What sets Christy apart isn't just her business expertise—it's her deep understanding of people. Whether it's decoding the human dynamics that drive success or simplifying money moves that lead to growth, Christy's hands-on approach makes her advice actionable and impactful. Her signature style—equal parts practical wisdom and motivating energy—shines through every page, leaving readers feeling ready to tackle their biggest goals with confidence.

Beyond business, Christy is a competitive dancer and dedicated volunteer, driven by her passion to empower others. She's actively involved in outreach and advisory board positions, including the Yelp Advisory Board, Innovative Women, and The International Trade Council. Through her advocacy with organizations like NORD and IDF, she's committed to creating positive change in the world.

For Christy, it's all about helping others achieve the success and fulfillment they deserve—whether in business, life, or their community. She's not just giving you a business blueprint; she's offering you the tools to create a life and business you truly love.

Ready to take your business and life to the next stage? Dive into *Dollars & Sense-Abilities* and connect with Christy at www.nextlevelconnected.com to join her community of business builders who are ready to take their journey to the next level.

Stop Procrastination and Start Seeing Results

Feeling stuck? This guide is your go-to for tackling procrastination head-on. Discover practical, easy-to-follow steps to stop putting things off and start making real growth progress in your business. Perfect for those who want to turn their intentions into actions and see immediate results. Get ready to move forward with clarity and confidence!

http://bit.ly/4d4r5dZ

www.ingramcontent.com/pod-product-compliance
Lightning Source LLC
LaVergne TN
LVHW010102170826
845678LV00012B/2220

* 9 7 9 8 2 3 0 0 1 6 3 1 1 *